IMAGES
of America

SANTA CRUZ

CALIFORNIA

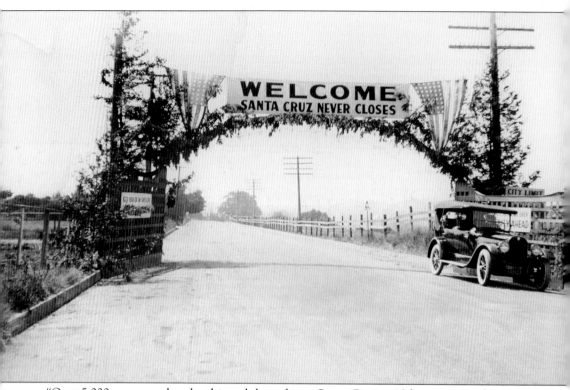

"Over 5,000 cars passed under this arch bound into Santa Cruz in 12 hours on Sunday, August 28, 1921." It was located at the northern city limits on Los Gatos Highway (at approximately today's Ocean and Plymouth Streets).

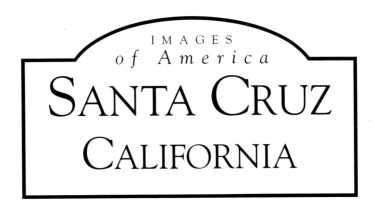

IMAGES
of America

SANTA CRUZ
CALIFORNIA

Sheila O'Hare and Irene Berry

ARCADIA

Published by Arcadia Publishing
Charleston SC, Chicago IL, Portsmouth NH, San Francisco CA

Printed in the United States of America

Library of Congress Catalog Card Number: 2002110144

For all general information contact Arcadia Publishing at:
Telephone 843-853-2070
Fax 843-853-0044
E-Mail sales@arcadiapublishing.com

For customer service and orders:
Toll-Free 1-888-313-2665

Visit us on the Internet at www.arcadiapublishing.com

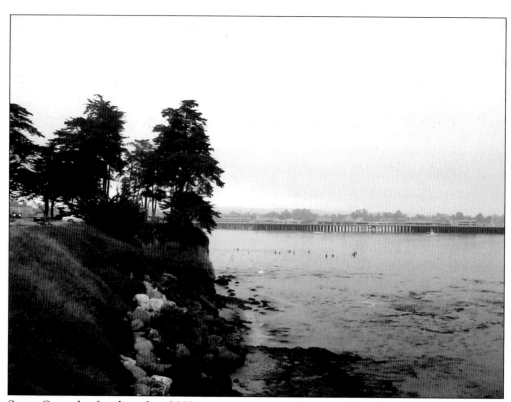

Santa Cruz wharf with surfers, 2002.

CONTENTS

ACKNOWLEDGMENTS

The authors would like to thank their colleagues at the University of California, Santa Cruz (UCSC) and acknowledge the staff of UCSC Special Collections for their assistance. The oral histories of Malio Stagnaro, Fred Wagner, Adalbert Wolff, John Dong, Henry Cardiff, Albretto Stoodley, Paul Johnston, Frank Blaisdell, Carrie Electa Lodge, Mr. and Mrs. Darrow Palmer, and Howell Rommel, all part of the UCSC Regional History Project, provided details in specific subject areas. Special recognition is due to: Don Harris and Victor Schiffrin at UCSC Photo Services; Andrew Phipps and Wayne Grim for technical support; and contributors Janet Young, Annette Marines, and Nina Berry.

The authors are grateful for the aid they received from members of the local history and genealogy community in Santa Cruz, and historians elsewhere: Al Crawley, Shirley Greenwood, Judy Yaeger Jones, Joanne Nelson, Marion Pokriots, Phil Reader, Stanley D. Stevens (UCSC librarian emeritus and curator of the Hihn-Younger Collection), Carolyn Swift, and the Researchers Anonymous group of the Santa Cruz Museum of Art and History.

Unfortunately, layout considerations do not allow us to include a full bibliography, but the authors would like to recognize works by the following authors: Richard Beal, John Chase, Geoffrey Dunn, Ross Gibson, Margaret Koch, L.G. Olin, Alverda Orlando, Tish Payne, Phil Reader, Leon Rowland, Carolyn Swift, and Jennie and Denzil Verardo. Particular mention is owed to the valuable indices to the *Santa Cruz Sentinel*, *Santa Cruz Surf*, and *Santa Cruz Evening News*, all of which were prepared by the Friends of the Santa Cruz Public Library. The Genealogical Society of Santa Cruz County's indices, especially those related to Burial Permits, are also noteworthy. Finally, the excellent and thorough local history section of the Santa Cruz Public Library web site and the *Santa Cruz County History Journal* provide more detailed information about some of the subjects included in this book.

Pictured below are three people who deserve special attention. Far left: Preston Sawyer as a young man. His personal collection, comprising his own photographs, collected historical photographs, memorabilia, personal scrapbooks, film, souvenirs and other evidence of a long and rich life in Santa Cruz and the surrounding area, was the kernel of the existing UCSC historical photograph collection. Second from left: Esther Rice, in her Santa Cruz High School letter sweater, *c.* 1920. She is responsible for a major part of what researchers know about these photographs through her tireless work as a volunteer researcher, identifier of photograph subjects, and bridge to other knowledgeable long-time Santa Cruzans. Third from left: Ernest Otto, newspaper reporter and historian of Santa Cruz. His stories for the *Santa Cruz Sentinel*, most published in the early 20th century, are recognizable for their balanced treatment of the life of the local community and their attention to subjects out of the mainstream. Finally, fourth from left: a child views the work of past local historians in "Santa Cruz Yesterdays" articles, published in the *Santa Cruz Sentinel*. UCSC's McHugh scrapbooks and Leon Rowland scrapbooks of local history news are true assets to all historians of Santa Cruz.

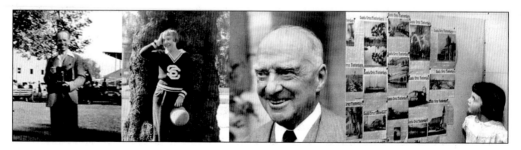

INTRODUCTION

"I am sure," said Helen, "a person ought to be happy in these woods. I never quite agree with myself which I prefer—the woods, the mountains, or the seashore. Here we have all three, and so even the most discontented person ought to be happy. For if a person feels weary of the sea, he can come up here and exchange the fresh sea breeze for the balsam odors of the woods. Is it not beautiful?"

—John Hamilton Gilmour,
"A Midsummer Idyl of Santa Cruz,"
Sunset, July 1909, pp. 70–76.

Helen, Gilmour's heroine, is quickly captivated by Santa Cruz. She is a young San Francisco stenographer who works in an "awful office." She needs to be somewhat economical in her vacation plans, but Santa Cruz is "just the place to have a good time. All you need is two or three good wash dresses . . . [and] a tent in the cottage city." She wants variety and liveliness (Santa Cruz "never gets monotonous as at other seaside resorts"), and she wants to consort with respectable people (her friend Arthur points out an "immensely wealthy" family, a "famous railroad man" and a "great financier" to her as they stroll about). Thus, between ocean bathing, dancing, fishing, good company, and walks among the redwoods, Helen's jangled city nerves are soothed and her spirits recharged.

Helen was not, of course, the only person enamored of the Santa Cruz area. Located on the Monterey Bay south of San Francisco and San Jose, its mild climate and natural resources drew entrepreneurs and visionaries as well as tourists. Over time, Santa Cruz became home to a classic seaside amusement park, the Boardwalk, with its Giant Dipper rollercoaster and Merry-Go-Round, both—unlike others of the era—still with us today. Luxury hotels and beachside mansions competed with cottage cities and revival camps. Captains of industry, writers, feminists and environmentalists, inventors, movie stars, criminals, demagogues, eccentrics, activists, and mountain men all made their homes there—and still do. The county has survived fires, earthquakes, floods, landslides, deforestation, and attempts at urban renewal. It created the Santa Cruz Venetian Water Carnivals, the Miss California Pageant (and the Myth California anti-Pageant), the Watsonville Apple Annual, the Capitola Begonia Festival, as well as other home-grown spectaculars in honor of everything from the Sequoia to the squid. In other words, the area and its people were and are ideally suited to avoid the monotonous.

The Ohlone or Costanoan, a Native American tribe that settled the coast from today's Marin County to Monterey County, first populated what is now Santa Cruz County. In 1791, Father Fermin de Lasuen established the Mission Santa Cruz or "Holy Cross." It was the 12th California mission. Around the same time, the Spanish founded Villa de Branciforte across the San Lorenzo River as a civil settlement or pueblo; the area is now East Santa Cruz. Based on prior negative experiences, the Franciscans insisted on at least a league of land between a mission and a pueblo, but this was ignored in Santa Cruz. The unruly Branciforte pueblo, earthquakes, floods, and the Mission's excessive restrictions on the native population all contributed to the Mission's demise; it was one of the first missions to be secularized. Mexico assumed control of the area by the 1820s, and Villa de Branciforte later merged with the Mission Santa Cruz community.

"Americans" found their way to Santa Cruz by the 1840s, and their numbers accelerated with the Gold Rush and California statehood in 1850. Santa Cruz County was also created in 1850 as one of the new State of California's original counties. The original focal point of Mission Santa Cruz was quickly overtaken by booming industry in the county: logging, limestone quarries, tanneries, and gunpowder manufacture were early successes. The city of Santa Cruz was incorporated in 1866 as a town under the laws of the State of California and received its city charter in 1876. Agricultural production began to play an increasing role in the 1880s, including dairy and poultry farms in Santa Cruz and, in South County, apple orchards, artichoke and strawberry farms, and nurseries. Commercial fishing expanded around 1900, bringing canneries and related businesses to the area. Moreover, promoters realized that the Helens and Arthurs of San Francisco, not to mention their counterparts elsewhere, might enjoy a visit to a relaxed yet prosperous town—close to nature but full of the latest conveniences, and blessedly far from the inland valley heat. Tourism loomed ever larger in the economic life of the area as Santa's Cruz's natural resources were depleted one by one.

Much, but not all, of this story will be outlined in the photographs included in this book. The authors were constrained by a number of factors: first and foremost by the need for a visual record. Some events, people, and things were never preserved photographically, or if they were, they are not yet accessible. Their absence gives an unfair advantage to the images we do have; it's all too easy to "whitewash" the past, and while we cannot redress the problem, it bears mention. Further, since the majority of the photographs in this book are drawn from the Special Collections of the University of California, Santa Cruz (UCSC), we are constrained by the limits of what has come to that collection over the years. The UCSC's holdings of local photography are excellent through the early 1930s, particularly thanks to the Preston Sawyer collection, but post-1940 photographic images are comparatively underrepresented in the collection. This has inevitably limited our scope, but it is equally certain that the collection will continue to grow as the popular definition of "historical" begins to encompass the later decades of the 20th century.

We have included some of our favorite lesser-known characters and events, but we also felt compelled to include others because of their well-recognized roles in Santa Cruz's past. We hope to have successfully "split the difference" so that both visitors to Santa Cruz and long-time residents can both find something to enjoy in this book. Finally, we have selected various images that depict Santa Cruz as a region—county as well as city—because of the importance of the relationship of many communities in the area's growth. It is a small county, closely bound by more than geography. A city like Watsonville truly deserves its own volume in this series, and there is much more to say about Capitola, Aptos, Davenport, and many of the other communities that make up the "Santa Cruz" area. ("Father" Riker's Holy City, located on Highway 17 just north of the Santa Cruz County line, is the only non-county site included; as a stopover that owed its existence to coast-bound travelers, it came to be associated with Santa Cruz rather than its own Santa Clara County.)

We have tried to show some of the less-idyllic moments in Santa Cruz history as well as the booster's paradise (the latter is reflected in the chapter titles, which are taken from 19th century promotional literature). Indeed, one of the best things about Santa Cruz is the way it has continued to evolve and learn from, if not to atone for, the errors of the past. It values natural beauty, accepts creativity and even eccentricity, encourages citizen involvement and activism, and, above all, recognizes the worth of its unique history, even if a little belatedly at times. The extraordinarily dedicated local history community of Santa Cruz has contributed immeasurably to the community's understanding of itself and its history, from the sublime to the ridiculous. This place is extraordinarily varied, and it has never been dull, not for a moment.

On the Acknowledgements page, we have attempted to thank the many people who contributed to the production of this book. A few special thanks, however, must be included here for those persons whose contributions were less easy to pinpoint, but who nonetheless made it possible to realize the entire project. For their willingness, inspiration, and good humor we thank the McHenry Library Reference and Collection Planning Departments, especially Frank Gravier and Christine Bunting. Donald P. O'Hare and Rita O'Hare provided much-needed encouragement, advice, and support from the project's inception to its completion. For Bob Berry, words of thanks seem too small to offer in return for "everything." Last, a special message goes to two Santa Cruz girls, born and bred, Nina and Helen Berry. To the "locals" of the next generation: this is your hometown.

One

A PLEASANT AND FRUITFUL LAND:

EARLY SANTA CRUZ

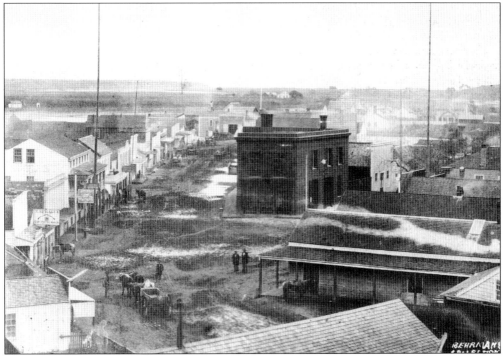

This view of downtown Santa Cruz is from the cliffs above Pacific Avenue at the head of Pacific and Front Street where they intersect Water Street. The photo can be dated to 1860, as a deed from August of that year refers to the flatiron building at center that had "just lately been completed by Hugo Hihn." According to local historian Ross Gibson, today's Front Street was called Main Street at the time that Willow Street (today's Pacific Avenue) began to grow. Originally Main Street was intended to run to the area known as Beach Hill, but too many orchards in its path needed river access for irrigation. The start of a shift of business to Pacific Avenue was the alleged reason for the shape of the flatiron building at the intersection: Hugo Hihn's design allowed him to hedge his bets on which street would prevail as the economic heart of the city. The flatiron building stood in continuous service as the city's oldest brick building until the 1989 Loma Prieta earthquake damaged it beyond salvation.

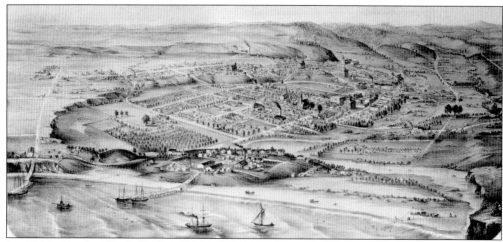

In 1876, Charles B. Gifford, a San Jose artist, drew this bird's eye view of Santa Cruz. Construction on the beach did not begin until 1877. A few of the major industries of early Santa Cruz are represented: two wharves, one the Bay Street Wharf and one belonging to the powder mill company, and lime kilns are indicated where the smoke rises in the center background. The bathing beach was at the mouth of the San Lorenzo River.

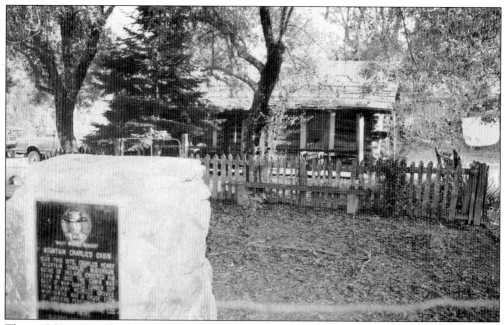

This is "Mountain Charlie's" cabin, 1996 (now a private residence). The monument inscription reads in part: "Near this site, Charles Henry McKiernan, native of Ireland, erected his cabin in 1850. The cabin was built of whip-sawed lumber cut from nearby redwood groves. Whip-sawing was a crude form of lumbering performed by two men, one in a pit under the log and the other above. McKiernan (1825–1892) came to the Santa Cruz Mountains in 1851. A not very successful hunter, rancher, and gold miner, McKiernan found prosperity in the 1870s with a stagecoach business; he also became famous as a colorful early pioneer who survived a grizzly bear attack in 1854. After the railroad diverted much of his business, McKiernan moved to San Jose in 1884. Mountain Charlie's nephew built the cabin in the early 1900s.

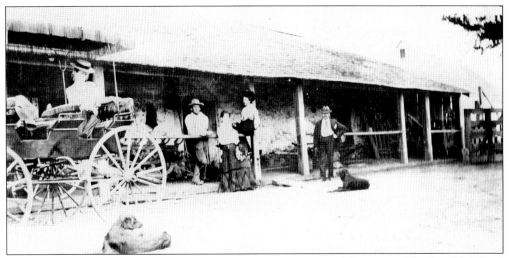

This three-room adobe house was built by Martina Castro and her second husband Michael Lodge c. 1833–1834 on her Soquel rancho. The Soquel grant in 1833 to Martina Castro of 1,668 acres was augmented by an 1844 grant of 32,702 acres. In the 1850s Castro was in effect bilked of her land in various dubious transactions. This photograph depicts the house on September 8, 1903, when it was used for storage on the Augustus Noble farm. The original thatched or tiled roof had been replaced by shingles. The structure, which had been built without nails (its timbers were tied with rawhide thongs), was torn down in the 1920s. The two men have been identified as Walter and Ed Noble; one of the three women is probably Walter's wife, Lilian McFarland.

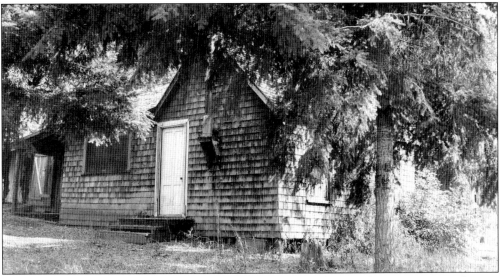

Isaac Graham built this house in 1843 as part of Rancho Zayante. Graham, a trapper, rifleman, and mountain man, settled in Santa Cruz County and made his living producing and selling whiskey. He recruited a band of riflemen to aid the successful 1836 revolt against the Mexican governor. The new governor, Juan Alvarado, may have learned a little too much about Graham and his associates: the next year he ordered the American foreigners arrested, and Graham and some others were sent to Mexico. Later released back to California, Graham returned to the Santa Cruz Mountains. In 1841, Graham and his partners erected a mill on Zayante Creek near the San Lorenzo River, reputed to be the first power sawmill in California.

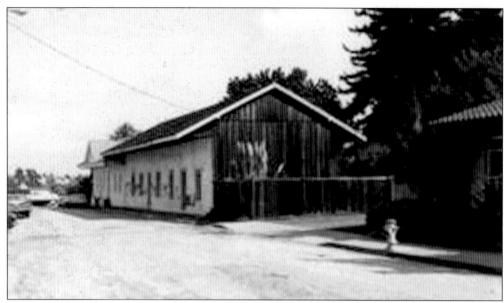

On September 25, 1791, the Mission Santa Cruz was formally founded as the 12th California Mission. Sometimes referred to as "the hard luck mission," it suffered through two floods before it was rebuilt on a hill overlooking the city. In the 19th century it fell into disrepair, losing its bell tower in 1840 and then collapsing in an 1857 earthquake. This part of the Mission buildings, known as the Neary-Rodriguez adobe, is the only section surviving from the 1791 original. It has been substantially restored since the time of this photo and is now part of the Santa Cruz Mission State Historic Park.

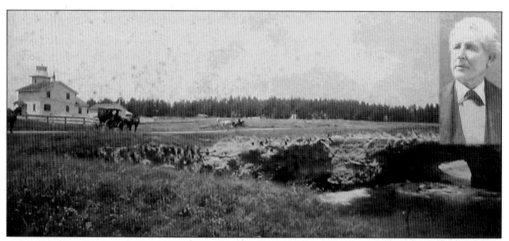

Adna Andress Hecox (1806–1883) was an early Santa Cruz pioneer. Grocer, alcalde, justice of the peace, county treasurer, and lighthouse keeper, Hecox arrived in California in 1846 and settled in Santa Cruz in 1848. His daughter, Laura, took over the lighthouse keeper position upon Adna's retirement in 1883; she kept the job for 33 years and died in 1919. Her collection of artifacts and shells formed the nucleus of the City of Santa Cruz Museum. The lighthouse, pictured in 1883, existed from 1869 to 1941. In 1967, the Mark Abbott Memorial Lighthouse went up at the site, a new brick building with a cupola designed exactly like original lighthouse. The Santa Cruz Surfing Museum, housed within the Lighthouse on West Cliff Drive, houses memorabilia from the lengthy surfing history of Santa Cruz.

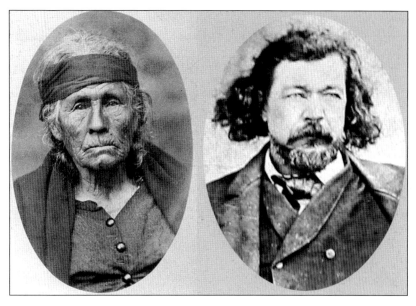

Early residents of Santa Cruz sometimes acquired almost legendary status. At left, Maria Josefa Perez y Rodriguez (1806–1890) was known as "Old Mother Chapar" or "Old Chepa" in later life. Often misidentified as a Mission Indian centenarian, she was in fact born at the Pueblo de Branciforte, a village overlooking the east bank of the San Lorenzo River. Married to Gervasio Soto and the mother of seven children, she and her husband were banished from Branciforte in 1842 for petty thievery and disorderly conduct. She returned to Santa Cruz in the 1860s and became a prime source for tales of the Indians and Californios. At right, Captain Harry Love in his only known photograph, taken c. 1862 in Santa Cruz. Love, a captain of the State Rangers, claimed to have killed outlaw Joaquin Murrieta in 1853. In 1855, Love moved to the San Lorenzo Valley area and married "Widow" Bennett, whose family had established a sawmill there in 1848. He logged the area until he was killed by Christian Ivorson, also a resident of the Santa Cruz Mountains, in 1868.

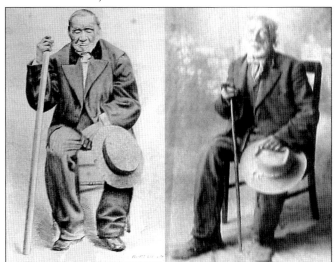

Justiniano Roxas (?–1875) was an Ohlone Indian born in Santa Cruz County. Popular myths about Roxas, including the story that he lived to be 123 years old, were perpetuated by W.W. Elliott's promotional volume, *Illustrations of Santa Cruz County* (1879). By the 1870s, California communities liked to promote themselves as possessing amazingly old Native American residents. Roxas' rumored 123 years actually came from a conflation of two or three people of the same name. Elliott's book features a lithograph image of Roxas (at left), depicting a nicely-dressed man with striped trousers and straw hat. A rare photograph of Roxas (right), used by the lithographer to create his image, reveals that his true labor-worn clothing and pose were extensively revised in the illustration process. The real Roxas spoke Spanish and an Ohlone dialect, kept very much to himself, and probably lived for 20 years in a county poorhouse.

13

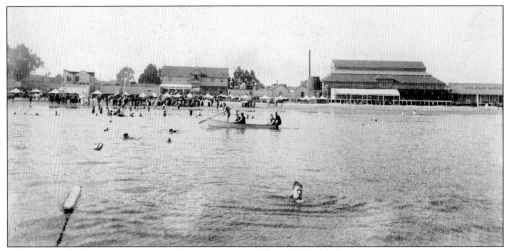

This view was photographed from the raft, a floating diving platform about 300 feet from shore, c. 1890. The line and floats that tied the raft to land are visible at left, and the beginnings of a tourist industry at the main beach in Santa Cruz before the existence of the Boardwalk are visible. John Leibbrandt built the Dolphin Bath House (at right), swimming tank, and entertainment house in 1868. In 1884, Capt. C.F. Miller opened the Neptune Baths (left of center). Leibbrandt and Miller joined their facilities in 1893 and built a bathhouse with an indoor seawater pool. The year 1894 was a turning point in Santa Cruz's tourism industry when an article in the national periodical *Harper's Weekly* promoted the area.

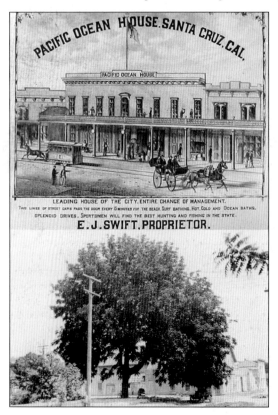

This black walnut tree, pictured at bottom c. 1920, is all that remains of Pacific Ocean House, a historic hotel built in 1866—the first local hotel entirely lighted by gas. The hotel had 150 rooms by 1892, and its own vehicle to meet incoming steamers and trains to bring guests to its doors. Its lack of an ocean view was balanced by its luxury and in-house amenities. By 1900 newer hotels were more popular, and it had become a boarding house. Its last section was demolished in 1962. The tree, however, still stands behind the site, a reminder of the elegant gardens of earlier times.

Nineteenth century Santa Cruz was home to a number of women writers. Top left: Eliza Farnham (1815–1864), reformer and writer, came to Santa Cruz in 1850 and farmed a 200-acre ranch left to her by her first husband for the next 11 years. Her book *California Indoors and Out* (1856) includes descriptions of "the peerless little valley of Santa Cruz," the struggles of pioneer farm families to make an adequate living, and the beneficial influence of women in California's pioneer society (over 90 percent

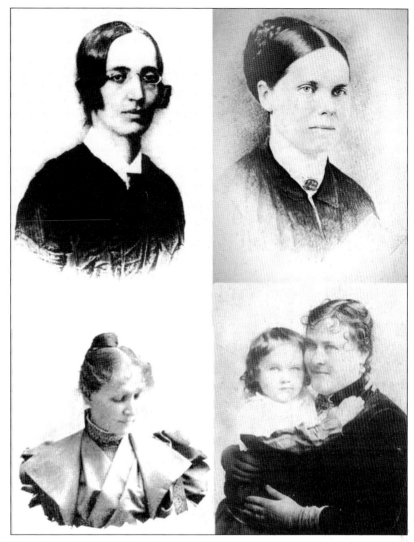

male in 1850). Top right: Georgiana Bruce Kirby (1818–1887). Kirby, an avowed abolitionist and political activist, followed her friend Eliza Farnham to Santa Cruz, where she married tannery owner Richard Kirby and settled permanently; her home at 117 Jordan Street still stands. She organized the Santa Cruz Society of Suffragists in 1869 and helped engineer the 1871 challenge to the California law prohibiting women from voting. Bottom left: Mary Hallock Foote (1847–1938), illustrator and author, married a mining engineer in 1876 and lived in many western states in the course of her husband's career. In 1877 they lived in Santa Cruz, where Georgiana Kirby befriended her. Bottom right: Laura Redden Searing (1839–1923), pictured with her daughter Elsa (later McGinn). Searing, deaf from age 11 and an advocate of both sign and speech instruction for the deaf, was a Civil War and foreign correspondent, newspaper editor, and poet under the pen name Howard Glyndon. After leaving an unhappy marriage, she resided in Santa Cruz at 138 Bay Street from 1886 to 1896 and survived by taking in boarders. Elsa's marriage to a man of means eased Searing's later days considerably. Her books of poetry include *The Hills of Santa Cruz* and *Of Santa Cruz*; a new edition of her poetry is forthcoming from Gallaudet Press, and a biography by Judy Yaeger Jones is in progress. (Photo courtesy Laura Redden Searing Papers, University of Missouri.)

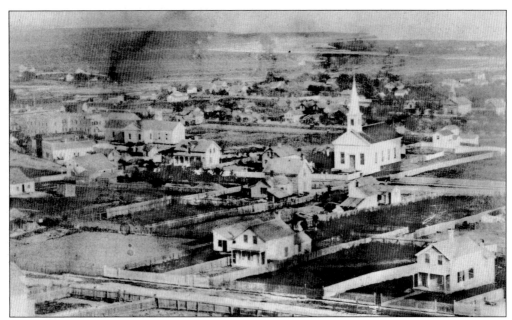

Santa Cruz *c.* 1866 was a small rural community. The steepled church at center right is the old Methodist Church at Green and Mission Streets. The schoolhouse is the building at left center; the middle part of the one-story structure was the original (1857) one-room school building. The two wings were added in the 1860s. The home in the foreground was owned by a milliner, Kate Handley. The home at center with veranda was erected by James Leslie in 1864.

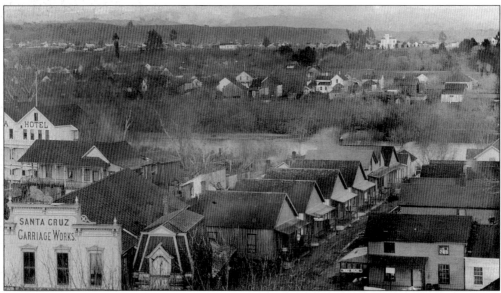

The first Santa Cruz Chinatown, pictured, was located on Front Street; it was destroyed in the 1894 fire. Later Chinatowns existed on Pacific Avenue and Bellevue Place. The original Chinatown housed small businesses, boarding houses, and three popular gambling houses offering keno and lottery games. Most of the Chinatown buildings were of rough redwood finish and board-and-batten construction. Note Santa Cruz Carriage Works at front left and snow on Loma Prieta in the background.

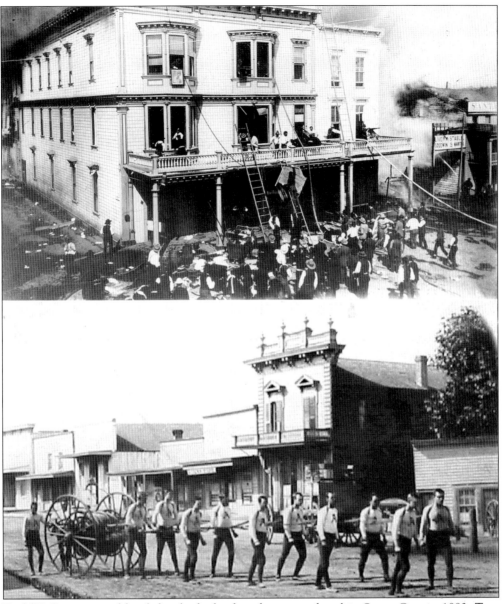

Fred W. Swanton and his father built the first three-story hotel in Santa Cruz in 1883. Top: The Swanton House, located on Front Street near the current Santa Cruz Post Office, burned a few years later on May 30, 1887. It was then the tallest building in Santa Cruz, and the fire-fighting hose teams of the day were unable to save it. Bottom: The Alert Hose Company Team, c. 1887. Hose cart races were popular sports contests in the 1880s; Santa Cruz had five volunteer hose cart companies (the Alerts, the Pilots, the Pogonips, the Kirby Company, and the Reliefs) and one hook and ladder company. They held races with other central county towns, the prize being a diamond belt that still remains in Watsonville today. Harry Cowell, son of the head of Cowell Lime Company, was one of the Alerts' lead men. Given the technology of the day, physical strength in itself could not always prevail; for example, the ornate two-story building behind the team, the onetime Germania Hotel, was destroyed by fire in 1894, along with much of the rest of downtown.

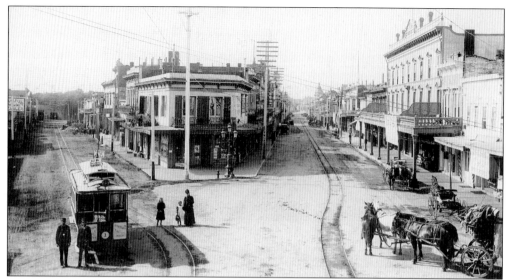

By 1894, the downtown area around the flatiron building had been altered by electric streetcar tracks (installed in 1891), utility poles, and larger, more elegant building facades. The streetcar at left is car number one of the Santa Cruz, Garfield Park, and Capitola Electric Railway. The shape of the area would be altered later that year by the great downtown fire, one of the many destructive conflagrations in the city's history.

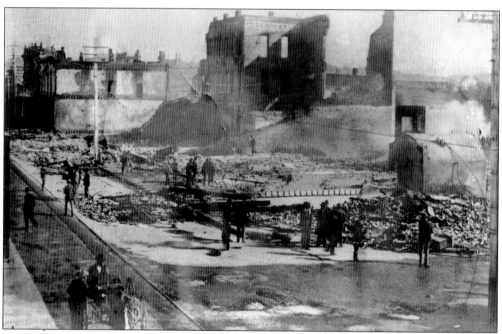

The downtown fire of April 14, 1894, broke out at approximately 10:40 on a Saturday night; earlier the same day, the city's water mains had broken and the water had been turned off, so water pressure was low. As this photo of the aftermath indicates, most of the large block bounded by Cooper Street, Pacific Avenue, and Front Street was consumed. The fire ended the city's reliance on volunteer hose teams. A paid fire department was established in October 1894 and a firehouse was built on Church Street.

18

Two
An Infinite Number of
Very Large Pines:
The Forest

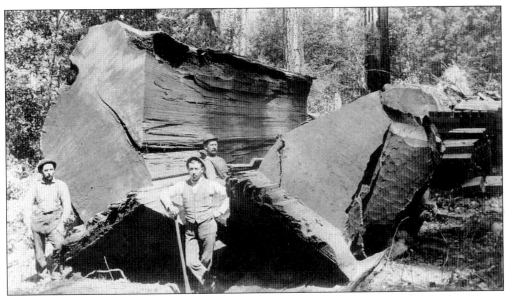

This redwood, cut in the Big Basin area above Boulder Creek c. 1900, was 14 feet in diameter—some harvested redwoods were 21 feet. This cabinet card was part of a series of logging images by E.B. Andrews of Santa Cruz. It was taken on property belonging to Maddock & McAbee; one of the owners actually homesteaded inside the Big Basin. Tom Maddock, a tan bark stripper, moved his wife and children into the Big Basin in 1877 and in 1882 filed a homestead claim to the land, reportedly obtaining 160 acres of virgin redwood forest for the filing fee of $7.50.

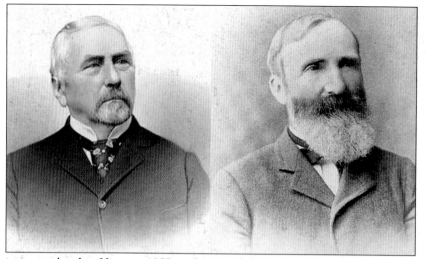

Frederick A. Hihn (1829–1913) (left), civic leader, businessman, and real estate developer, arrived in California in 1849. He opened a mercantile store in 1851 in Santa Cruz, turned it over to brother Hugo in 1857, and proceeded to amass a fortune in real estate holdings. At one point Hihn owned one-sixth of the county. His lumber enterprises may have left the biggest mark on the county; however, he also founded the town of Capitola, constructed railroad and horsecar lines, formed the first water system in the county, organized the city bank, and served as county supervisor and member of the state assembly. Charles Bruce Younger Sr. (1831–1907) (right) was Hihn's principal attorney and was engaged in nearly all the important land and railroad litigation in early Santa Cruz County. The Hihn and Younger families were joined by the marriage of Hihn's daughter Agnes to Younger's son, C.B. Younger Jr. The Hihn-Younger Collection at UCSC is an invaluable source for the early life of Santa Cruz, including maps, business and personal correspondence, and artifacts.

F.A. Hihn's residence, "a monument to the taste and good judgment of the owner" (Santa Cruz County, California Illustrations, 1879) and supplied with gas, hot and cold water, was built in 1872 at 75 Church Street. It was acquired by the city around 1920 for use as the City Hall, but was demolished in 1938 and replaced by the existing city government center.

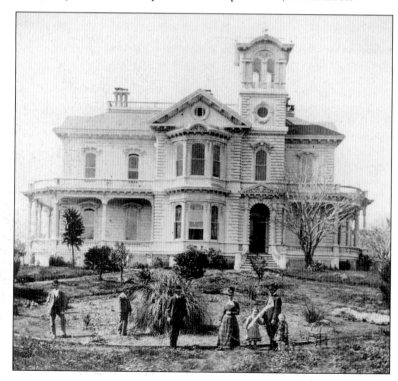

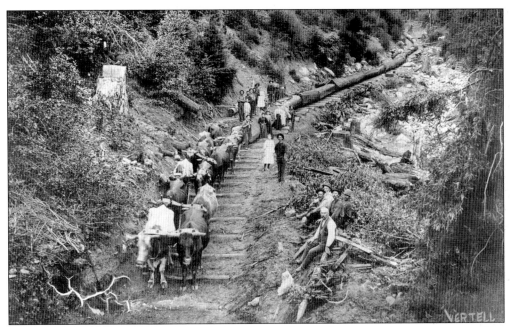

Ox teams were used to drag logs over skid roads to mills, a risky process that meant controlling the slide of the heavy logs to keep them from rolling into the oxen. This scene from the Santa Cruz Mountains was taken behind today's Brookdale Lodge (built 1890), two miles south of Boulder Creek. Stephen Grover, the man in the white shirt, was the owner of the Grover Lumber Mill; the bull driver, back at right next to the animals, is Chris Iffert; and the girl at center is probably Lillie Grover.

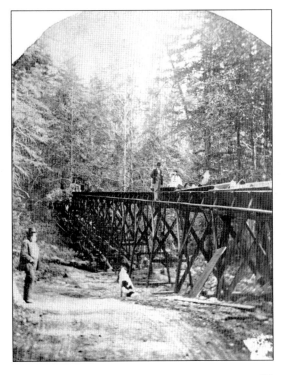

A 13-mile long flume built from Felton to the headwaters of the San Lorenzo River was completed in 1868, and the railroad began to run from Santa Cruz to Felton in 1875 and from Santa Cruz to Boulder Creek by 1885. The same backers paid $165,000 to build this flume, designed to carry lumber to the railroad from a point miles up the Valley, before the railroad could reach that remote location. Each segment was floated down along the previously built section to its completion. The job of flume walker was to constantly walk the line to prevent pileups. Water to float the lumber came from a dam near the top of the line at Two Bar Creek and Clear Creek, near today's Brookdale. When the railroad reached Boulder Creek, the day of the flume was over. This section is likely between Waterman Gap and Felton, late in 1890. The original photograph bears the notation "showing 'boats and passengers,' " a possible reference to the practice of flume riding.

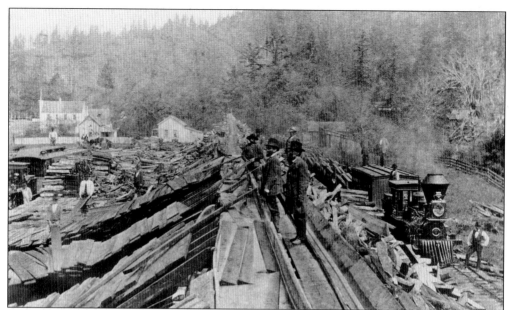

This is the sorting and sizing yard at the railhead of the Santa Cruz & Felton Railroad, at the foot of the San Lorenzo Valley flume, in the late 1870s. Two engines served the line, the Santa Cruz (left) and the Felton (right). Logging industry growth in the upper San Lorenzo Valley was spurred by the construction of the lumber flume from north of Boulder Creek to Felton in 1875. It was torn down in 1884 and replaced by a railroad line.

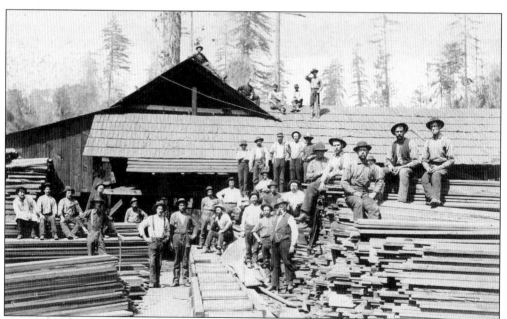

Pictured is Grover's Mill, north of Soquel, with Stephen Grover at front (white mustache) and a group of his workmen. Grover and his three sons logged in many locations in the county, including Soquel, Bates Creek, Porter Gulch, Brookdale, and the area above Boulder Creek. About 20–25 men worked in a sawmill; they boarded in town for the winter in places like the Swiss Hotel, the Railroad Exchange, and the Garibaldi, and were credited with keeping many saloons in business.

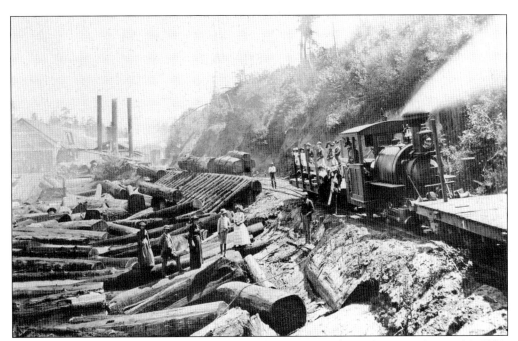

The engine was called "Betsey Jane II," and the location was above Aptos on August 14, 1891. The name honors the first Betsey Jane (1873), a tiny wood-fueled locomotive owned by the Santa Cruz Railroad Company that was used in the construction of the company's narrow gauge line between Santa Cruz and Watsonville.

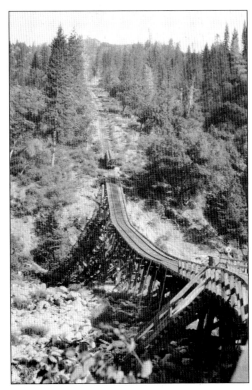

The Molino Timber Co. was organized to log a tract of redwood lumber owned in the Loma Prieta forest area north of Aptos. This lumber had not been harvested previously because of the difficult terrain. However, split logs could be transported by a narrow gauge railroad, which was cheaper and simpler to build than a standard gauge railroad. The company used only one small locomotive above the incline, a 10.5-ton, 2-truck shay, one of the smallest logging shays ever used. The area was ruthlessly clear-cut over a 40 year period from 1883–1923 and is still recovering as Nisene Marks State Park.

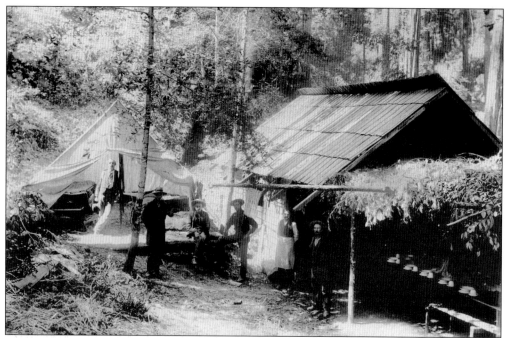

Tan bark oak trees were the source of tannic acid for the leather industry in Santa Cruz. Massive quantities of tan bark were needed. Trees were felled in spring, marked off in four-foot lengths, and hacked in rings to loosen the bark, which were then peeled off with an iron "spud." Pictured is a tan bark camp in Big Basin in 1895. Winfield Scott Rodgers is under the tent in the photo.

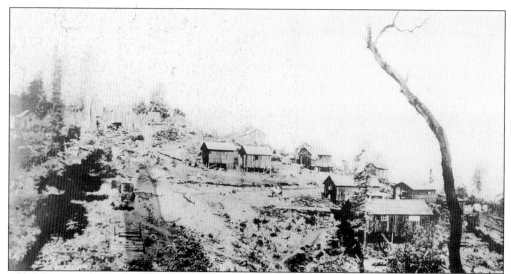

Not much was left after logging in the early days. The original photograph reads, "Shacks of Loma Prieta Camp on Railroad Grade"; the photographer was documenting the buildings, not the view. The Loma Prieta Lumber Company, according to the oral history of worker Albretto Stoodley, "took all the redwood that was of marketable size"; no seed trees were spared unless they were simply too small to be saleable. Moving the logs out of the area meant burning the area in preparation for the construction of a greased "skid road" down the gullies to the mill site. This rare photo depicts the effects of late 19th and early 20th century lumbering.

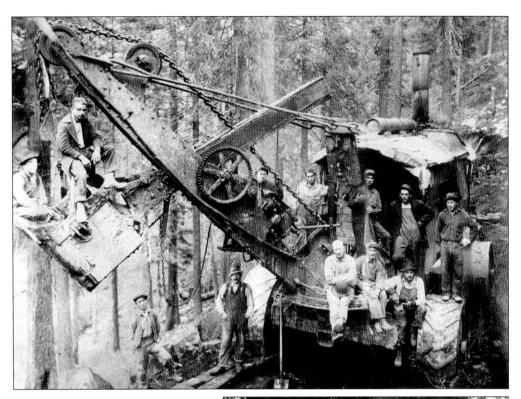

Logging crews like this one worked on a seasonal basis, since the rain and mud of winter made their work too difficult. Heavy equipment for log hauling eventually replaced oxen. A "donkey engine" was a large stationary steam engine with a vertical boiler and heavy drums to wind up the wire cables that dragged in the logs, beginning the move to larger equipment.

Boulder Creek redwoods provided work for George Cress, the man on the left in this photo. Cress arrived in Boulder Creek in 1905 after mining gold in Alaska for four years. He worked in the lumber industry and then in tourism, opening the Moody & Cress Livery Stable with Fred Moody. Cress would meet trains in the morning, pick up campers and their equipment, deliver them to tent cabins, and then make the trip back to the train with returning customers.

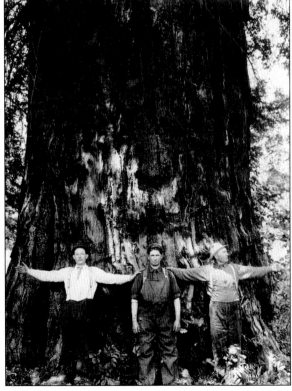

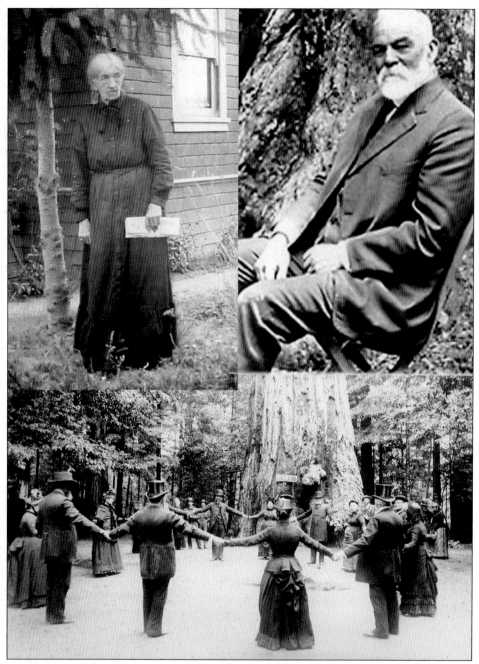

How to demonstrate the sheer enormity of these mighty living things? One method is shown here, in a photo taken at "Big Trees Grove" (later Big Basin). The redwood trees of Santa Cruz—*sequoia sempervirens*—are among its greatest draws for visitors. The movement to "Save the Redwoods" started in Santa Cruz County, *c.* 1900. The efforts of Andrew Hill (1853–1922) (top right), Josephine Clifford McCrackin (1838–1920) (top left), and other members of the Sempervirens Club were instrumental in creating a redwoods state park. In 1901, some 3,800 acres at Big Basin became California's first state park, although a forest fire delayed its opening by several years. The Club's advocacy also led to the creation of the California State Parks system.

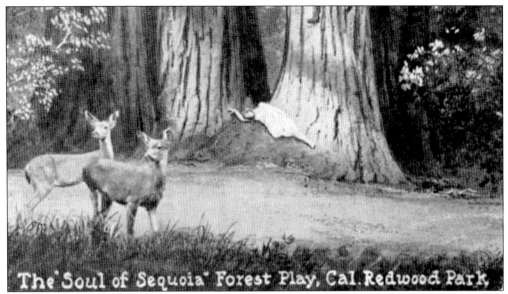

The Soul of Sequoia" Forest Play, Cal. Redwood Park.

In 1919, the Sempervirens Club presented the first annual outdoor forest play, "The Soul of Sequoia." The play was written and composed by Don W. Richards and Thomas V. Cator, and its theme "was carried on by aesthetic dances, vocal numbers and spoken words. . . . Among the leading actors was one of the mountain deer, which, lured by the calls of the assistant park warden, had been tamed sufficiently for the appearance in the play. "The play concluded with an episode in which the trees were saved from the woodman's axe. The spectacle so impressed one writer that he referred to it as "the Oberammergau of America," predicting that his city might be compared to the famous home of the Passion Play.

The custom of attaching notes to certain trees in Big Trees Grove may have had its origins in the folklore of the "wishing tree," or it may simply have been a non-destructive method for leaving graffiti. Lula Wood Sherer (later Neville), pictured, moved to Santa Cruz in 1907 with her husband Will, a photographer. Will Sherer's studio was located at 144 (now 1325) Pacific Avenue. Lula was frequently drafted into service as a model for her husband's souvenir shots. She died in 1974 at age 93.

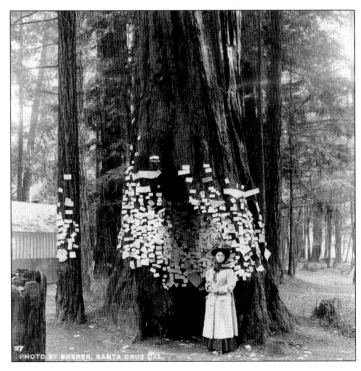

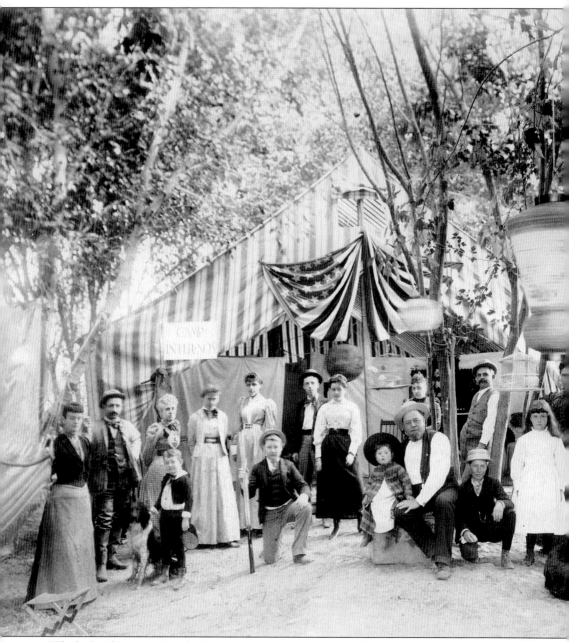

Whole families joined in the forest camping experience, including pets (note the dogs and the two birdcages). This group was in Boulder Creek.

Three

A Wealth of Industry:
Manufacturing

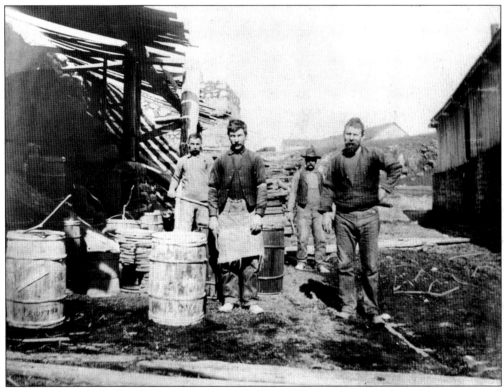

These workers are loading lime into barrels at the Cowell Ranch. Essential for making mortar and cement needed for construction, lime became one of the county's most lucrative early exports just as the state began to boom. Production began in earnest when two enterprising Americans, Albion P. Jordan and Isaac Davis, developed their facility in 1851 in time to supply the need. By 1878 it was bringing in $200,000 a year and producing about half the needed lime in the state, which was shipped out via its own wharf at Santa Cruz. Later sold to Henry Cowell, this was one of three such operations in the county. Many of the Cowell Ranch lime workers were Portuguese single men, and in 1915 they received $1 per day, plus food and living accommodations (described often as "shacks"). The shacks, as well as some of the kilns used in lime production, date back to the time of this photograph and still stand on the UCSC campus today.

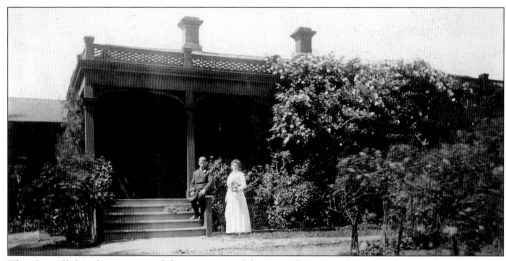

The Cowell family was one of the state's wealthiest and most private families, with interests in real estate throughout northern California and Washington State, including commercial buildings, ranches, limestone quarries, cement mills, and timber tracts. Santa Cruz was just one of the places to benefit by its generosity, not only by the establishment of the University of California's ninth campus on the Cowell Ranch lands, but by Henry Cowell State Park as well, which was created as a memorial to his father by Samuel H. "Harry" Cowell. Although Henry and Harriet Cowell raised five children, there were no grandchildren, and much of the family's wealth went to the public good. Today the S.H. Cowell Foundation oversees grants for the benefit of youth and families, creation of affordable housing, and improvement of public education. Pictured are Henry Cowell and Edith Cowell Lane at the Cowell Ranch, High Street, Santa Cruz, about 1908.

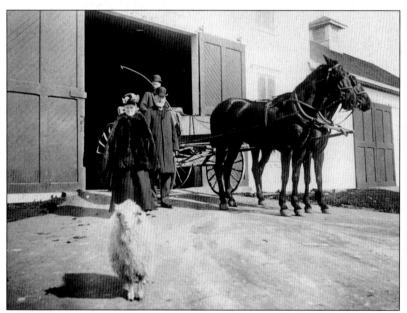

Mr. and Mrs. Henry Cowell stand in front of their carriage house; Frank George is in the wagon, and a goat takes over the foreground. George (1868–1949) was a lifelong Cowell stableman and ranch manager; the Cowells kept an "immense" flock of goats, possibly to keep the brush down. The carriage house is now a suite of offices on the UCSC campus. Like other ranch buildings, it was adapted as-is architecturally, so that the appearance of the original ranch would be maintained.

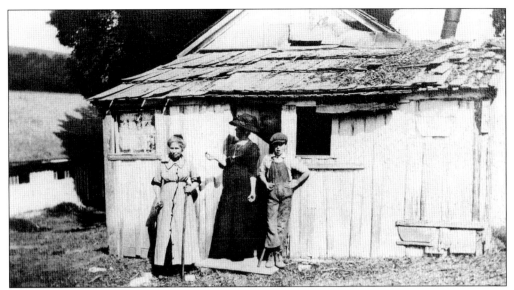

Small buildings like these, which served as housing for the workers at Cowell Ranch, still dot the hillside at the UCSC campus entrance. Pictured here c. 1900–1905 are Mary Hickey Shaw, a Santa Cruz native born in the pioneer era c. 1860; her sister Nellie Hickey Rubottom; and her son, Roy E. Shaw.

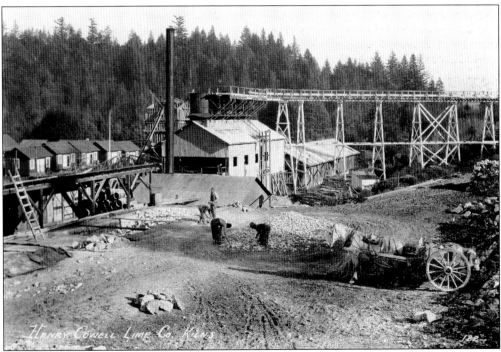

Rincon was one of several sites in Felton that produced lime. More than just the right kind of geology was needed to support lime production: wood was needed in vast amounts to fire up the kilns that let the processing take place, and the San Lorenzo Valley was fortunately situated to provide both lime and forest land. This placed the industry in direct competition with area sawmills for the same limited resources.

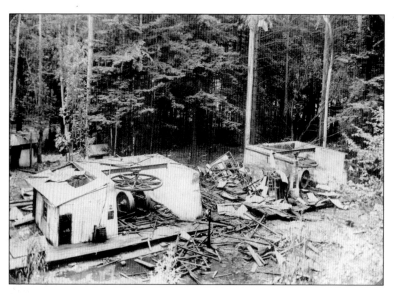

The California Powder Works were established when the Civil War prompted both an increase in production of explosives and in expenses for black powder that had to come "around the Horn" at a cost of about $20 per keg. Beginning in May 1864, the California Powder Works turned out some 150,000 25 lb. kegs. Despite safety precautions, explosions did happen. The accident pictured above took place on October 21, 1905, when wheel mills No. 1 and 2 blew up; fortunately, there were no injuries, though the crew on duty had a narrow escape. To minimize damage in the event of mishaps, the design of the plant called for many small buildings well separated over some 200 acres. After this event, the thick concrete walls left standing were reincorporated when the buildings were rebuilt.

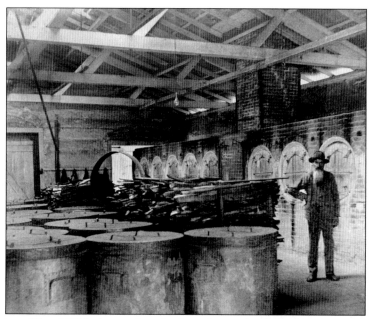

Louis Abraham Manseau (1829–1916), pictured in his place of work, was a powder maker. "Boss of the retorts" at California Powder Works, he oversaw the process by which wood was converted to charcoal, a vital component in the production of explosives. As the first company on the Pacific coast to produce nitro-cotton smokeless powder for cannons, CPW was one of two suppliers to the U.S. government during the Spanish-American War. CPW also produced prismatic powder for high-power breech-loading cannons, and it was known for having supplied powder for the Pacific and Asiatic fleets of the U.S. and for Pacific harbor and shore defenses in the 1800s. However, CPW never did produce dynamite, which changed the explosives industry. In 1906, it was acquired by DuPont, production was moved to Hercules in 1914, and in 1924 the site was sold to the Masonic Lodge and became Paradise Park, a riverside residential area.

This is the guncotton mixer at the California Powder Mills, 1901. Smokeless powder was produced primarily from guncotton, a substance produced by treating cotton with nitric acid, resulting in nitrocellulose. This is also the basis of celluloid, an early plastic. One of the workmen is John Jensen.

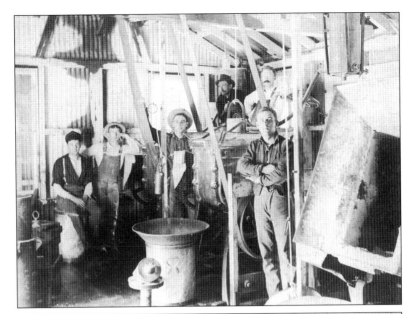

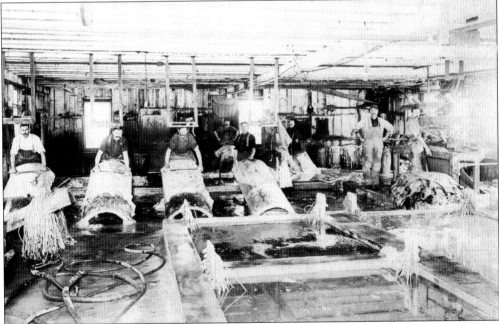

Tanning was another of the county's early profitable industries. Driven by an increased need for leather materials for traditional uses, success for local tanneries was ensured by the rising industrial economy: specifically, the need for drive belts for the machinery in many new factories built around the country. By 1870 there were nine tanneries in the county, generating some $382,000 per year in income. Chief among them was this tannery, built by James Duncan and William Warren near the San Lorenzo River in 1856. Rebuilt after flooding in 1861–62, it was purchased by Jacob Kron in 1866, and produced 250 sides of sole leather per day. In 1918, it became the Salz Tannery, which remained in business until 2001. The other tanneries declined with the loss of the area's tan bark oak tree, provider of the necessary compound for the tanning process—removal of the bark killed the trees.

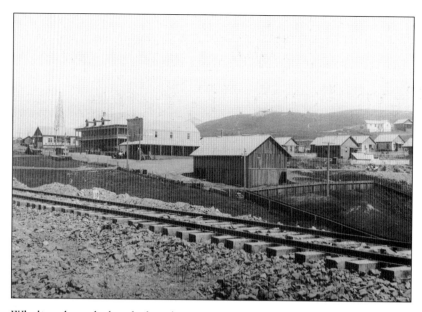

The Davenport cement plant was built by the Santa Cruz Portland Cement Company in 1907. Davenport became an important shipping point with the construction of a wharf at the site of its whaling operations in the 1860s.

Whaling there declined after about 1875, but its attractive location for shipping ensured it would continue to thrive for some years until competing shipping points came into being. Lime from nearby quarries was shipped out of Davenport Landing until 1905; in 1907, the new Santa Cruz Portland Cement Company constructed a cement plant about a mile south of the old landing location. The Davenport plant eventually became one of the largest suppliers of cement in the world, shipping out 700,000 barrels a day after World War II. It is still in operation, although technology and environmental practices have changed substantially since the days when local children broke off chunks of the thick white cement dust that formed to use for sidewalk chalk.

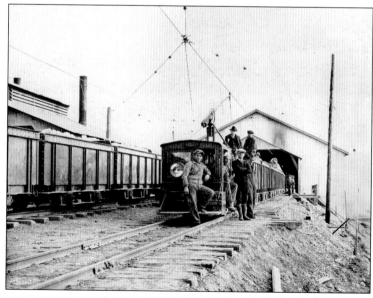

The cement plant began Davenport's era of growth. Santa Cruz rejected the idea of a cement plant as too noisy and dusty in 1903, and "Cement King" William J. Dingee decided instead to locate the plant 10 miles up the coast at Davenport in 1905. Davenport had its own cement plant railroad system. Beginning in 1905 a steam engine ran on a standard gauge line from the cement plant to the quarry, and on a narrow gauge line in the quarry open pit. In the 1920s an electric narrow gauge line replaced this system.

Four

THE BEST TONIC:
THE BEACH AND
THE BOARDWALK

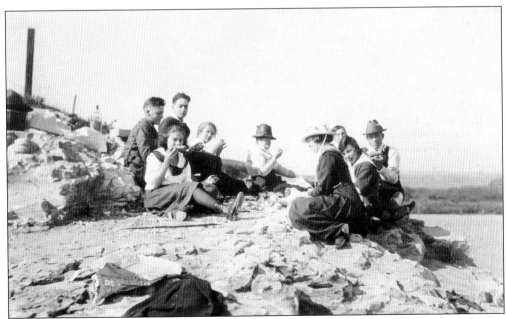

Moore's beach is today's Natural Bridges State Park Beach, though the sand bridges and caves of earlier years are now gone. This picnic group of November 10, 1918, includes Ariel Sawyer (third from left), photographer Preston Sawyer's brother, who later had a local theatrical career; he performed in a novelty vaudeville act in 1921 entitled "Chicken—and Old Hen" at the New Santa Cruz Theatre. Hazel Van Dyke, on the far left, is the dancer featured in a later photo in this book. The other participants are members of the Stratton and Hoover families.

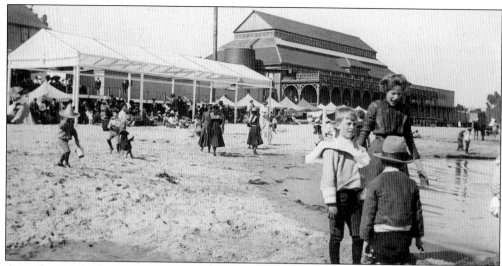

According to the *Santa Cruz Surf* in 1885, surf bathing in the town allegedly began in the early 1860s with an impulse plunge by Sam Drennan and John T. Porter. They so enjoyed its invigorating effects that their accounts inspired a group of gentlemen and ladies to secure a coach (which the ladies used as a dressing room) and drive to the beach for an ocean plunge. Thereafter, small changing rooms were constructed as bathing joined hunting and fishing as a popular vacation activity, culminating eventually in Leibbrandt's Bath House and its successors.

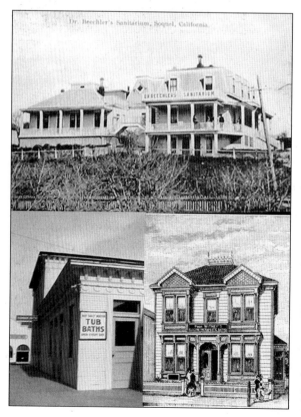

The Mediterranean climate and salt water of Santa Cruz made it a natural location for turn-of-the-century therapeutic resorts. By 1864 hot saltwater bathhouses appeared on Beach Street offering rheumatism and neuralgia treatment. Bottom left: Mary Jane Hanly's Salt Water Baths. Hanly was an English nurse who began her health care business at the beach and eventually moved to a building at Bay and West Cliff in 1924, which became the first hospital in Santa Cruz (Sisters Hospital). Bottom right: Professor Witney's Electric Baths, located on Pacific Avenue near Beach Hill. In 1883, before Santa Cruz had electricity, Witney offered hot tubs heated via batteries and a generator with mild electric currents running through them. A number of "electric cures" were popular in the era. Top: Beechler's Sanitarium in Soquel, which operated until 1915, was a converted Victorian mansion. It was lost in a 1930s fire.

Pictured are Fred W. Swanton (1862–1940), left, and Frank Fiester, installation men for the "new amplifying telephone" at Napa City, February 1884. As a young boy, Swanton moved to Santa Cruz from Brooklyn, New York in 1866. In the 1880s, he established the first telephone system in Santa Cruz. His early entry into the utility business linked Swanton to the capital required for his seaside developments. In partnership with Dr. H.H. Clark, Swanton formed the Santa Cruz Electric Light and Power Co. in 1890, bringing incandescent lighting to Santa Cruz over the objections of the city's political leadership. Six years later, the pair expanded their utility business with the creation of the Big Creek Power Co. By the time the two companies were sold to San Franciscan John Martin in 1906, they had expanded their power lines to Capitola and Watsonville.

The Boardwalk's original Neptune Casino, a Fred Swanton enterprise, opened in 1904. It was destroyed by fire 22 months later. Elements of its Moorish design were maintained in its 1907 replacement, which still stands today.

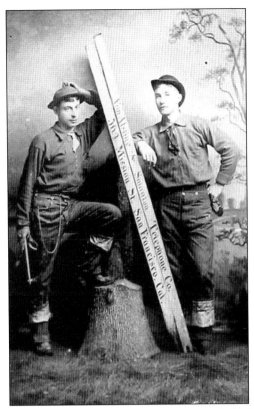

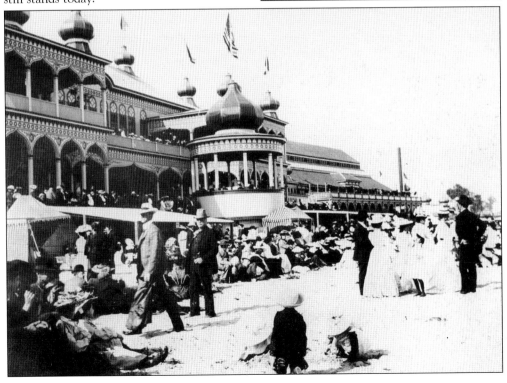

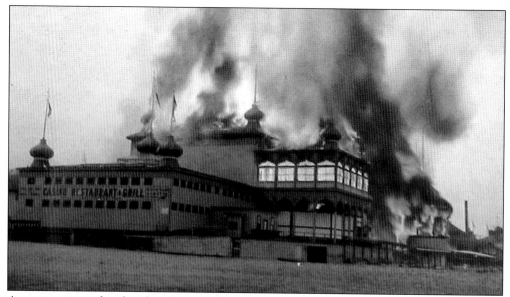

A mere two months after the 1906 San Francisco earthquake, Fred Swanton's Neptune Casino "burned to the sand" on June 22, 1906. The elegant structure was just two years old. Swanton's response to the disaster was to rent a circus tent and carry on with the summer tourist season while rebuilding a bigger, more grandiose casino. The newer structure opened in time for the following season, and—with some modifications—remains to the present day.

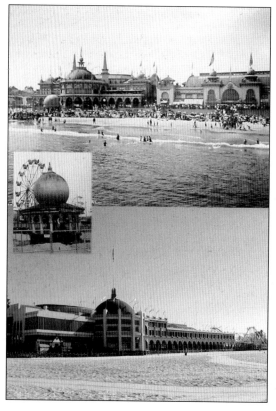

The rebuilt Boardwalk Casino of 1907 (top) is the building we know today, despite some changes to architectural details over the years; it is the last of the west coast seaside amusement arcades. A 1980s remodel brought a thorough updating, although like past modernizations it seemed to be made in the spirit of Fred Swanton's original. One of the authors remembers taking a camera one early morning to document the wholesale demolition of the old arched walkway, and finding one of the old landmark "onions" (inset) from the old rotunda placed on the sand behind a protective fence. Was it meant to be incorporated into the new design? Where is it today? The Casino today (bottom) is more popular than ever. Its perfectly groomed sand is the result of an agreement with the city to clean the sand in front of the Boardwalk—machines systematically sift and smooth it before the tourists arrive. A good part of the area in front of the casino looks as unmarred as a tabletop in the early mornings.

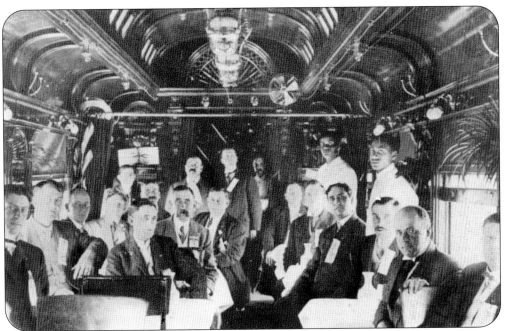

The Boardwalk and boosterism went hand-in-hand: pictured are Fred Swanton, Fred Howe, and others on an early "booster" excursion, c. 1909. Swanton began the current Boardwalk when he transformed the 19th-century Miller and Leibbrandt Bath House into a large-scale tourist attraction. By 1904, new construction at the Santa Cruz beach included a casino, pier, plunges, and a tent city for accommodations. Swanton promoted the "New Santa Cruz" by traveling throughout California and Nevada with members of the city's official booster committee and a marching band; his early trips were made in private railroad cars loaned by Southern Pacific. Over the next 25 years, he continued to visit small inland towns via automobile caravans, featuring parades, promotional giveaways, and concerts.

"Santa Cruz—Never a Dull Moment." So began Fred Swanton's sixth annual tour of Santa Cruz Boosters. Swanton, who became mayor of Santa Cruz for three consecutive terms, was an astute promoter; he used many of his train trips to bring the name of Santa Cruz to the public in California's Central Valley towns, an ideal clientele. Appropriately, one of the banners in the background reads, "Santa Cruz Says Eat

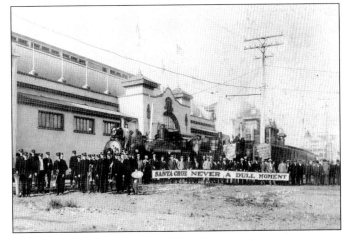

California Raisins." In April 1906, Swanton was quoted as follows in the *Santa Cruz Sentinel*: "Pajaro Valley has its apple crop, Santa Clara Valley its prune crop, Fresno its raisin crop, Bakersfield its grain crop and Santa Cruz has its crop of home-seekers and tourists. It is all-important that this crop be cared for."

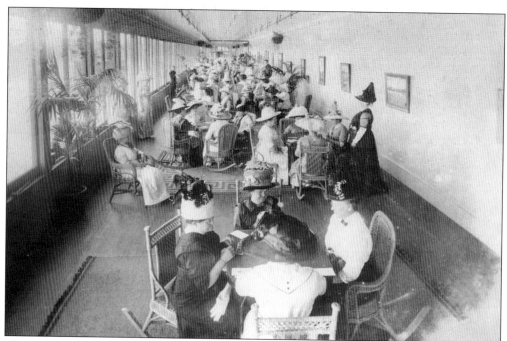

The second floor of the second Casino building on the Bay side included "Palm Court," a connecting hall from the ballroom to a point overlooking the Boardwalk.

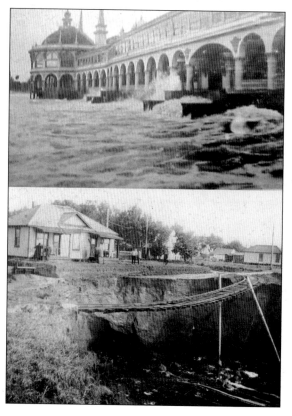

Weather-related beach disasters were not infrequent. At top, waves crash on Casino front side. In the winter of 1913–14, rainfall records were broken in many areas of northern California. Beach sand was gouged out to a depth of three feet under the Boardwalk. At the Casino itself, baseboards of the great rotunda were carried away and the bandstand was damaged. Allegedly, the post-storm area in front of the Casino was full of now-exposed valuables that had been buried in the sand, which local "prospectors" cheerfully recovered. At bottom: a washout on the Capitola electric trolley line, February 7, 1915, near Seabright. The Union Traction Company's line at the east end of Twin Lakes Beach ran over a long trestle built in 1904. In the 1915 winter storm, waves washed away a large section of bluff and left the tracks suspended in midair.

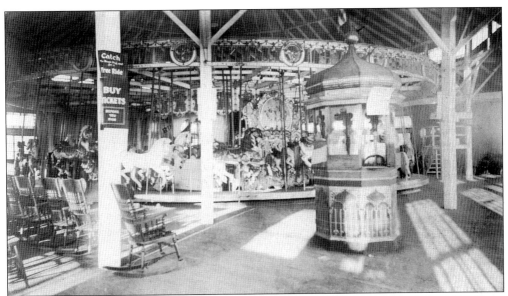

The Boardwalk is still the site of two rare attractions: the 1911 carousel and the 1924 Giant Dipper rollercoaster. Both were manufactured by members of the Looff family, early and prominent makers of amusement rides. Charles Looff designed the carousel; his son Arthur designed the rollercoaster. Rocking chairs were provided around the carousel for non-riders.

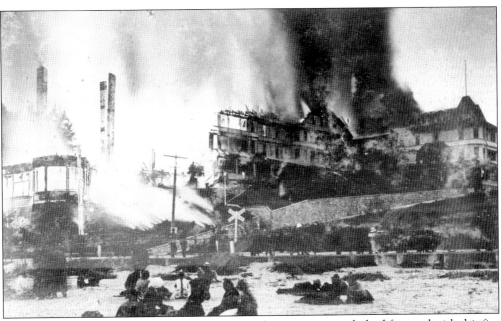

Hopes for Santa Cruz as a real world-class tourist destination were dashed for good with this fire on June 12, 1912. The Sea Beach Hotel was Santa Cruz's answer to Monterey's Del Monte Hotel. Built in the 1870s, it was enlarged in the 1880s, and was one of the state's top coastal resorts in the 1890s. It was known for its beautiful floral gardens. Guests included two U.S. presidents (Harrison and T. Roosevelt). Many Santa Cruz residents (see foreground) came out to view the inferno, which lasted over four hours. Halls running the length of the building were blamed for the rapidity of the fire's spread through the 170-room hotel.

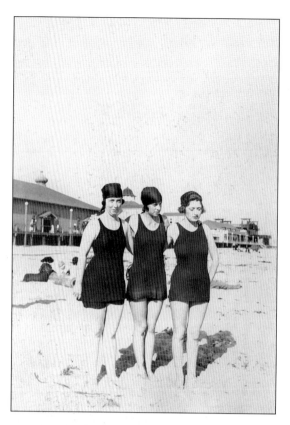

Pictured are three members of the Native Daughters, representing members of pioneer Santa Cruz families at the Native Sons Three Day Admission Day Celebration, c. September 1919. At left is Grace Hickey (later Nash), daughter of Mary Hickey (pictured earlier); center is Edith Williamson (later Kilfoyl), related to the Delameter and Wilder families. The *Santa Cruz Evening News* bemoaned the swimwear of the era in a 1923 article: "The bathing dress of a young lady, 30 or 40 years ago, came below the knees and had sleeves that reached to the wrist. This outfit was completed with stockings, a cap, and a straw hat. . . . This is quite different from the young flapper of today, with her one piece bathing suit and her desire to acquire a slick coat of tan."

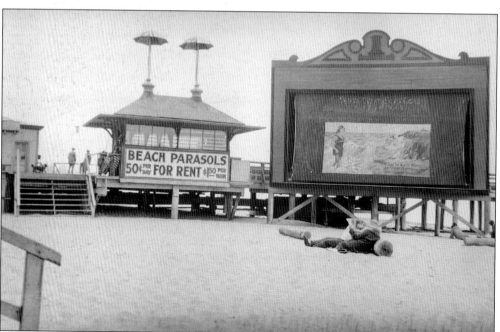

The Santa Cruz Beach Bandstand was located at the Boardwalk end of Pleasure Pier in the 1920s and '30s. It later moved to a site in front of the Merry-Go-Round.

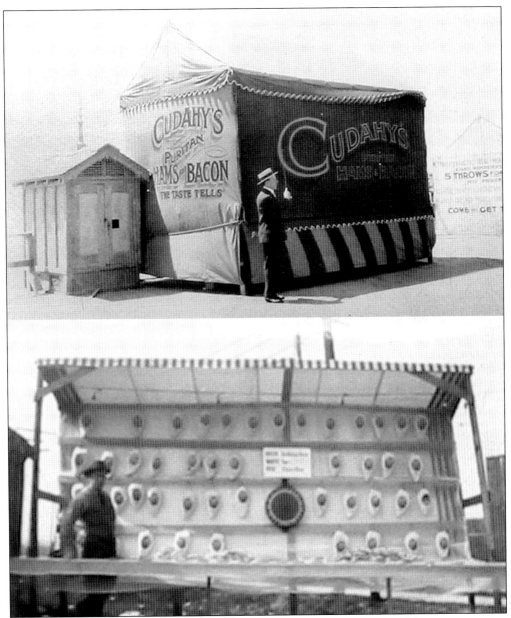

In the 1920s, Sam Haberman ("Sam the Ham Man") operated a ham and bacon concession named Cudahy's on the beach boardwalk. He later built cottage courts in the beach area. The Ham Stand was only one of Haberman's Boardwalk concessions, though it was probably the best known. Theme booths like "Happy Home" and "Around the World" were part of his 1927 roster, as well as the traditional "Milk Bottle" pyramid game—in this case with a background "designed especially to advertise Santa Cruz's milk and dairy industry."

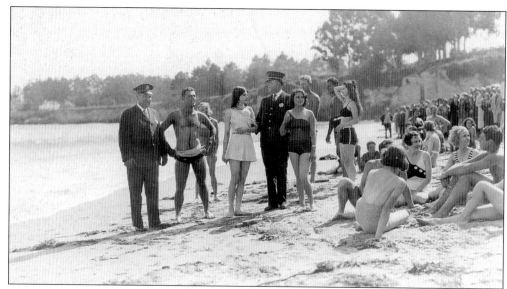

Cowell Beach was a popular spot for surfers. Surfers claimed the "Steamer's Lane" early on, and it remains a major destination today. Second from left is Hal Stuart, a lifeguard; fourth from left is William Walker, chief of police for Santa Cruz in 1929–30. In 1932, he pleaded guilty to accepting bribes from bootleggers while chief and served time in San Quentin. "Rolling down" swimsuits (presumably to avoid tan lines) was enough of a problem that in 1932 the city council held an exhibition of bathing suits to assist them in drafting "a law dictating what will constitute modesty for Santa Cruz beach this summer." (*Santa Cruz Evening News*)

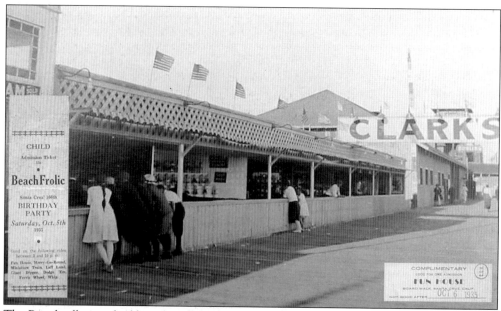

The Boardwalk once had boards. A segment of the old wooden walkway has been preserved for display near the Merry-Go-Round, but the surface of the Boardwalk today has been replaced by pavement. Concession game booths lined the walkway. Insets: Two Boardwalk tickets from the 1930s. The ticket on the left lists the Boardwalk attractions of the year: the Merry-Go-Round, Fun House, miniature train, Laff Land, Giant Dipper, Dodge 'em, Ferris Wheel, and The Whip.

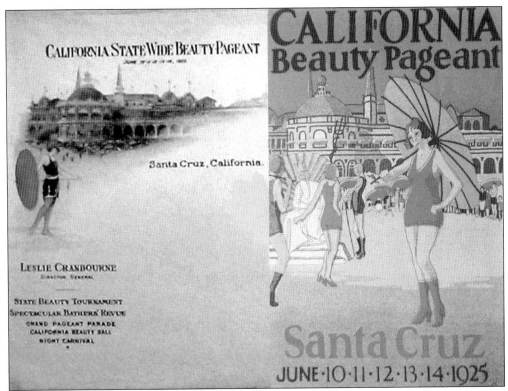

The California State Wide Beauty Pageant, later the Miss California Pageant, began in Santa Cruz in the 1920s. Another of Fred Swanton's promotional schemes, the first Miss California Pageant in 1924 was criticized for promoting heavy makeup and indecent clothing. However, the pageant survived and became the cornerstone of a week-long schedule of festivities including parades, dances, aquatic events, and mini-pageants (a Baby Venus and Baby Adonis were selected). The pageant left Santa Cruz in 1990, again under fire for promoting a controversial view of the feminine ideal.

Pictured is Miss California of 1924, Faye Lanphier, on the float entered by the Santa Cruz Beauty Pageant Directors in the California Raisin Day Parade at Fresno, April 30, 1925. The float won first prize for the best entry. Lanphier (inset, right top) was the first Miss California and was Miss America of 1925. Inset, left bottom: Beauty Pageant ephemera.

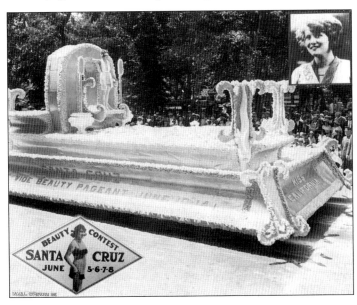

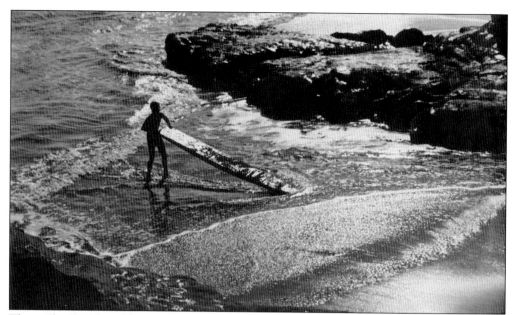

This surfing longboarder was photographed on February 14, 1943. Early 20th century California surfboards were often heavy redwood planks. The hollow board was introduced in 1928, and the mass production of lighter-weight boards (using a balsa wood-redwood combination) commenced in 1937. The first fiberglass surfboard was produced in 1946. Early surfers were impressive for their strength and endurance. As one of the northernmost popular surfing areas in California, Santa Cruz is considered frigid compared to most other major surfing regions, and wetsuits were not widely used before the mid-1960s.

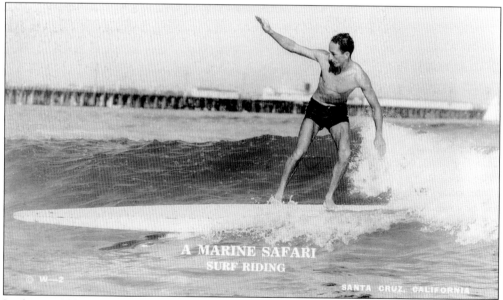

In the pre-1930s era, surfing in Santa Cruz was more of an acrobatic feat than a sport and was generally limited to exhibitions. However, even as more people took to the sport, water exhibition events remained popular in the 1930s and 1940s. The surfer here is Leland "Scorp" Evans, a surfer and snow skier of the pre-World War II era.

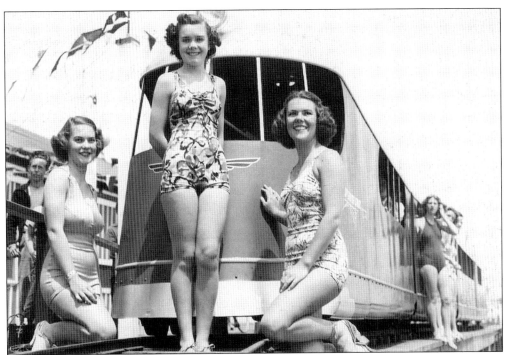

Boardwalk publicity photographs often incorporated the Miss California Pageant. Pictured at left is Cynthia Currell; at center, Miss Santa Cruz County of 1938, Gloria Daley.

Pictured is Donald E. Patterson (1907–1977), also known as "the Mighty Bosco," *Santa Cruz Sentinel* pressman, well-known aquanaut, and original Santa Cruz Surfing Club member. Water shows in the area were often capped with a 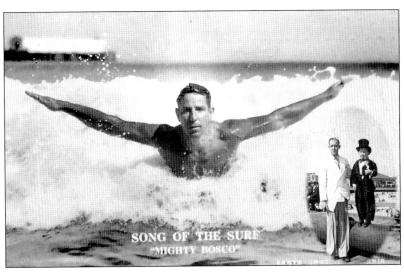 spectacular "fire dive" by the Mighty Bosco, who would wrap himself in old bathing suits and long johns, start himself on fire, and dive off a high platform at the plunge. He repeated this stunt on over 300 occasions at the Boardwalk. Inset at lower right: Warren "Skip" Littlefield in 1969, with "Eugene." Born in 1906, Littlefield began his association with the Boardwalk as a pin boy for a pitch game. His long career at the Boardwalk included 53 years as its publicist until his 1981 retirement. He promoted "Sun Tan Special" trains to Santa Cruz for 24 years, staged shows, dances, and plunge water carnivals (as well as Bosco's stunts), and became the greatest single source for Boardwalk history.

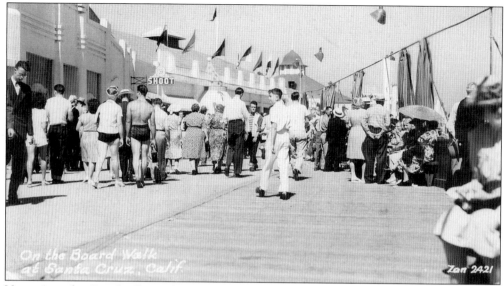

On the Board Walk at Santa Cruz, Calif. Zan 2421

Visitors to the Boardwalk in the age of legal liability will remember with a certain grim amazement the era of the Fun House. It is visible in this photo at center left behind the crowd by its huge clown face entrance (note the blackout curtains at right in this 1940s photo). It featured a high, polished wooden slide, with carpet scraps furnished by attendants to minimize the friction burn on the way down; a huge turntable that hurled riders off by centrifugal force; a spinning barrel tunnel with a sign warning takers to remove their glasses before entering; and a rocking, bucking "moving sidewalk" near the front windows. Air jets screamed up from the floor to surprise girls in a skirt-wearing era. For a quarter, a young visitor could almost spend the day there. To be a local is to have worked on the Boardwalk: one of the authors remembers enjoying employees' tales from the old Fun House and what one had to do to be "sentenced" to a shift in the place. It was torn down in the early 1970s.

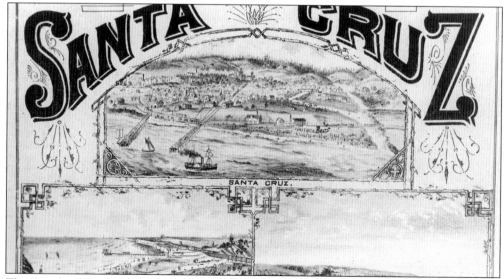

The Boardwalk in the 1940s offered "patriotic" games. Inset at left: As this Boardwalk ticket reflects, the "Sink a Nazi, Sink a Jap" game could be played by '40s visitors. This game was still playable as late as 1979, but was turned to the wall thereafter.

This crowd gathered for fireworks at the Boardwalk, July 4, 1950. Skee Roll (a game that uses heavy wooden balls that players roll and pitch up a slanted ramp into holes) and Pokerino have remained popular arcade games, pretty much unchanged, since they were installed in 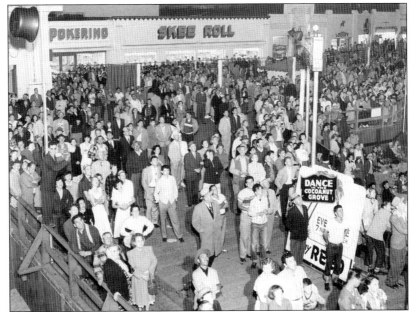 these locations. A fireworks show at the Boardwalk on July 4 was a community tradition through the mid-1970s, when the sheer size of the crowds, the bottlenecked traffic afterward and a sharp rise in crime ended it. Fireworks have returned to the skies above the Boardwalk in recent years, but for other community celebrations, not Independence Day.

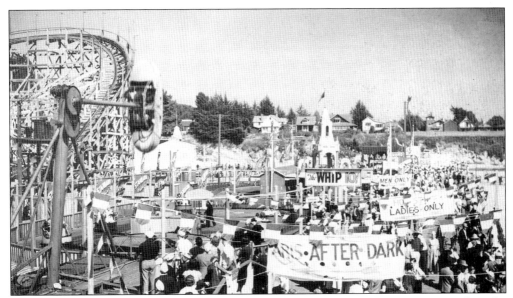

This is a later view of the seaside amusement park in the postwar era. In recent years, when the Boardwalk was struggling to reposition itself as a wholesome family destination, and at a time when amusement parks in general were plagued by flagging attendance, it was this era it was trying to live down. By the 1950s and '60s, as an older attraction, it had acquired an aura of seediness and ill repair. (Note the signs that read "Paris after Dark," "Hot Stuff Ladies Only" and "Men Only.") Disneyland and other theme parks offered cleaner, newer, more up-to-date facilities and a less rowdy clientele.

49

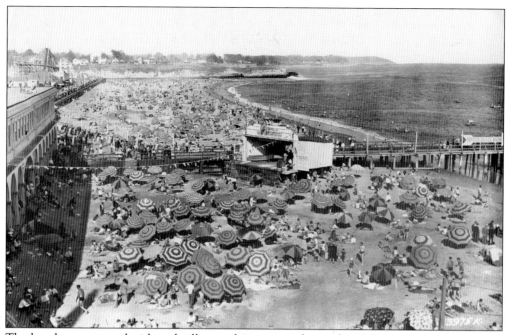

The beach was covered with umbrellas on this summer day in the 1950s.

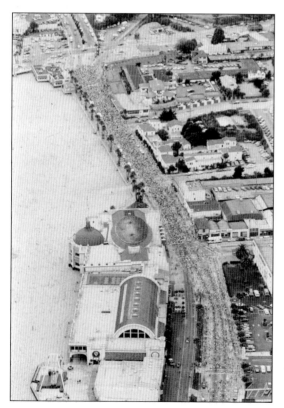

This aerial view of the Boardwalk in the 1980s also depicts runners in the Wharf to Wharf Race. First run in 1973, the Wharf to Wharf Race is a popular road race along a six-mile, oceanside course stretching from the Santa Cruz Wharf to the Capitola Wharf. Held every year on the fourth Sunday in July, the race benefits local athletic organizations.

Five

BRIGHT WATERS:
THE WATERFRONT

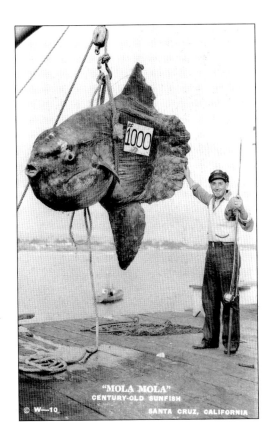

"MOLA MOLA"
CENTURY-OLD SUNFISH

© W—10

SANTA CRUZ, CALIFORNIA

In June 1940, Sammy Pennington captured a giant sunfish weighing 1,400 lbs. in the bay on the north coast. The fish was displayed for spectators at the Stagnaro market. Its near-circular shape, and the fact that sunfish in the area seldom weighed over 10 pounds, made this postcard image very popular with both locals and tourists.

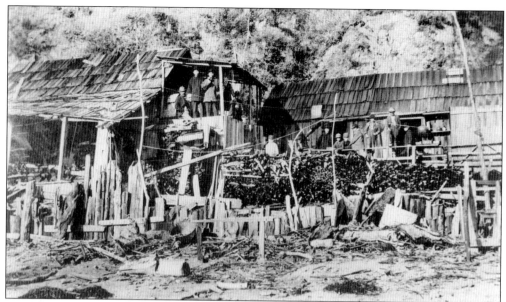

China Beach (or China Cove) was a Chinese fishing colony around the point east of Capitola, c. 1880. In the summer of 1880, 29 men resided there, selling fish to tourists on site or peddling them door-to-door. Technically they were squatters, and the colony had disappeared by 1900.

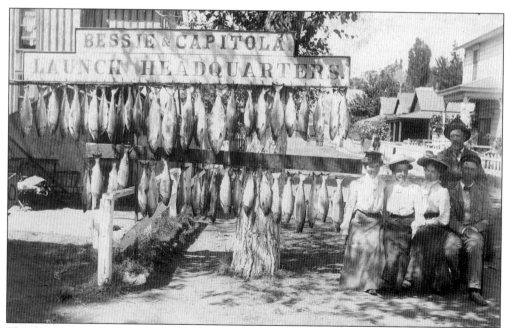

The day's catch of salmon for Bessie & Capitola Launch Headquarters, Capitola, 1880s. With the completion of the Santa Cruz Railroad, fish could be caught in Capitola and shipped to San Francisco markets on the same day—thus encouraging the development of the industry.

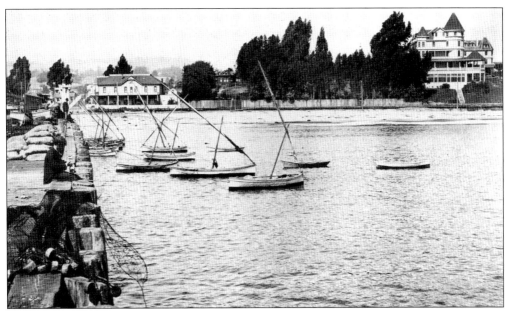

These lateen rig boats are viewed from Railroad Wharf, c. 1900. Lateen boats had prows fore and aft, could be rowed or sailed, and were manned by two-man crews. These fishing boats were commonly used from 1900–1910 by the group of Genovese fishing families (Stagnaros, Ghios, Loeros, Bregantes) who settled in the Bay Street-Laguna Street-Gharkey Street area of Santa Cruz. Also visible are the Old Sea Beach Hotel (right) and St. James Hotel, later the Il Trovatore Hotel (left, facing wharf).

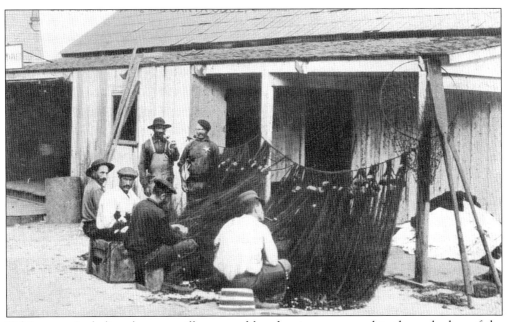

Fishing nets including dragnets, gill nets, and beach seines were used in the early days of the Santa Cruz fishing industry, c. 1900–1910. Initially, women made the nets by hand, earning $8 per net, and producing one net a week with day and night work. This lasted until the late 1920s–1930s, when machine-made nets came into use.

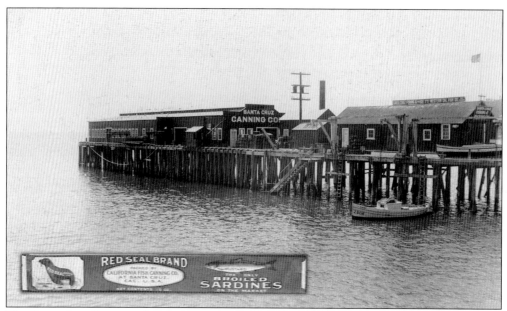

The Santa Cruz Canning Company operated on the outer end of the railroad wharf in the late 1910s and early 1920s. It was a branch of a plant operating on lower Washington Street. The smaller building on the wharf at right was then the local office of the Western California Fish Company of San Francisco. The wharf was dismantled beginning in late 1922. Inset: Company label from a collection of business-related ephemera in UCSC's Special Collections, which preserves many such "disposable" items of everyday life.

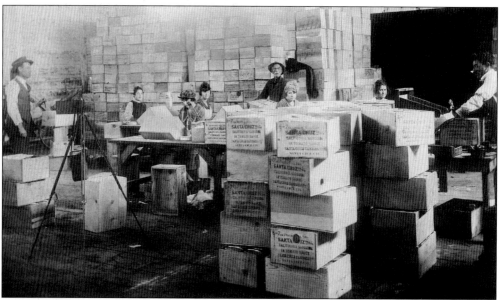

Santa Cruz had two fish canneries—one on Washington Street (with a second location on the wharf) and one beyond Twin Lakes Beach. For a short time an abalone cannery operated on Vine Street. This photograph has been identified as depicting the Washington Street cannery in the 1920s. The boxes read: "Santa Cruz California Sardines in Tomato Sauce, Santa Cruz Canning, Santa Cruz, CA."

54

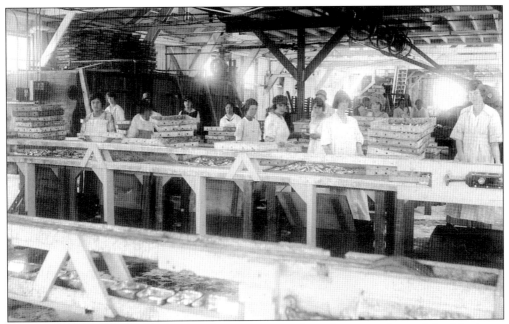

Young women employees of a local sardine cannery go about their everyday work in this photo. The majority of all workers in the California canneries were women; their jobs required little formal training.

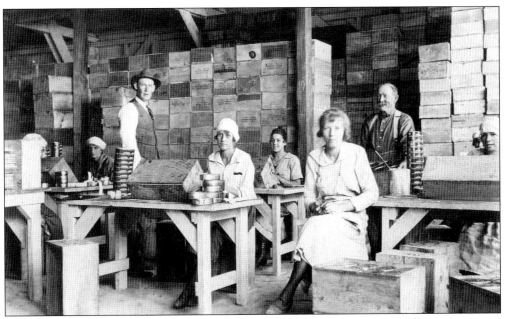

Post-World War I, Santa Cruz's fish canneries moved to Monterey. Sardines were more available on that side of the bay; moreover, the canneries drew multiple complaints related to their smell and refuse dumping practices. Outlets from the cleaning benches in the canneries were releasing oil and fish scum into the bay, with obvious negative effects on surf bathing (not to mention the woolen bathing suits of the time). This may explain the salt-water "plunge" swimming pool located directly adjacent to the ocean.

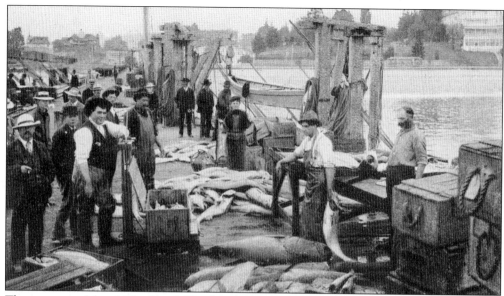

The presence of the old Sea Beach Hotel in the background at right dates this morning scene on the old railroad wharf to pre-1912. In the early 1900s, Santa Cruz developed a fishing industry both for local trade and for the markets of San Francisco. Fish would be packed "round" (not cleaned), iced, and shipped by rail in boxes weighing 150-200 pounds. These shipments to San Francisco were made on consignment, adding an element of uncertainty to the industry. Left foreground: Louis "Jim" Perez; two men on right are "Lallino" Bregante and Willie Silva; boy facing the camera at center is Steven Ghio, who died a year or two later at San Diego when caught in a burning fishing boat.

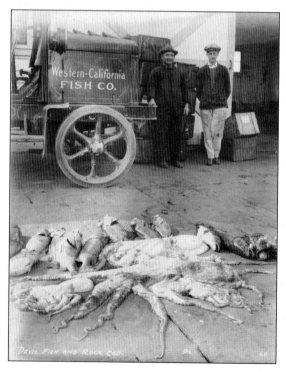

San Francisco fish dealers began to send their own trucks to and set up branch operations in Santa Cruz to purchase and transport fish, c. 1914. This truck belonged to Western California Fish Company, a San Francisco concern; other dealers with Santa Cruz branches included San Francisco International Fish Company and Standard Fish Company. The man on the left is Domenico "Sunday" Faraola, who operated a retail market on the railroad wharf as well as peddling fish locally via a local horse-and-wagon operation.

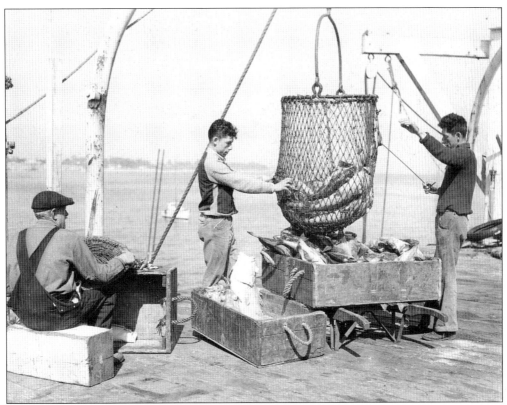

The new Santa Cruz Municipal Wharf was opened at the end of 1914; the *Pacific Marine Review* enthused that "[w]ith its construction the first opportunity in many years is presented for an outlet by water for the industrial products raised and manufactured in the City and County of Santa Cruz." The article went on to note that fish shipments out of Santa Cruz amounted to three million pounds annually. In the center of the photo is Joseph E. Stagnaro; at left is R. "Stago" Stagnaro.

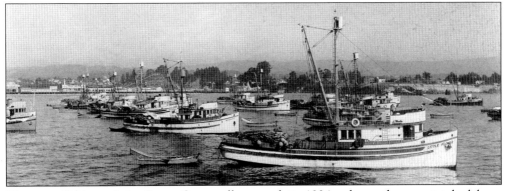

The tuna fishing era in Santa Cruz really started in 1934, when other species had been overfished to near-extinction. The boats are, from front to back: *Little Flower, Western Maid, Vagabond, Virginia B., Sea Lion,* and *Giant Dipper.*

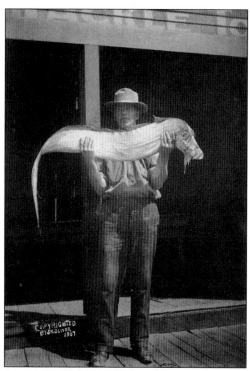

Local newspapers reported many strange catches in Monterey Bay, one being this "ribbon fish," c. 1907. Other recorded examples include a "violin fish," the name again descriptive of its shape, and an outright "sea monster," later tentatively identified as the skin of a rare whale.

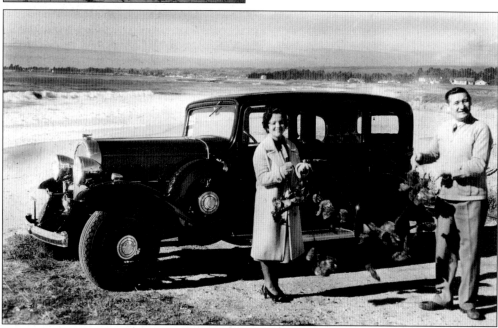

Pictured is George Goebel, who purchased a fish market at the approach to the municipal wharf in 1923. The Goebel Market sold fish and game, fishing bait and tackle, and groceries. Goebel and the unidentified woman may be holding Japanese oysters grown on a rope. Oysters were introduced and cultured in the county beginning in the early 1900s. Unfortunately, they were also the transport mechanism for a Japanese mudsnail—an ecologically troublesome exotic invader species.

Six

THE PLEASURE GROUND
OF THOUSANDS:
TOURISM

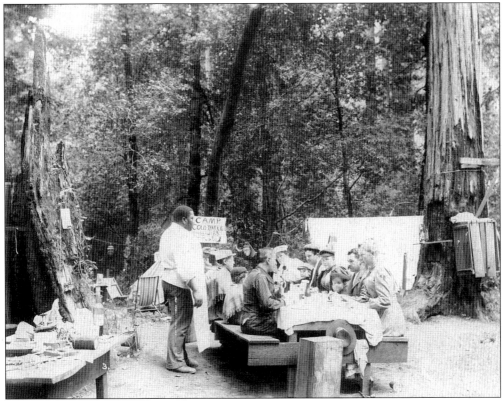

The sign reads "Camp Coldwater," and the cook at left is Albert Logan (1860–1922), who began his culinary career in the sawmill camps. The sawmill camps were known for serving excellent food to attract workers, a policy since the 1880s. In 1896 Logan and his wife Mary converted a home on S. Branciforte to a boardinghouse for African-American visitors, which operated for the next 50 years.

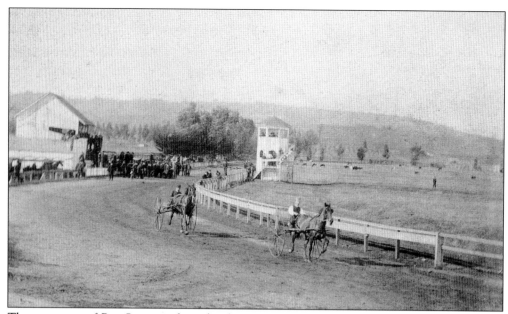

The area west of Bay Street and south of Mission Street became known as the horse racing district beginning in the 1860s. A professional, mile-long racetrack was built on West Cliff Drive between Swift and Fair Avenue. It opened early in the 1870s, with a tavern, betting parlor, and hotel, and became tremendously popular with both locals and tourists. The horses raced were pacers, so it was sometimes referred to as the Bay View Trotting Track. After the 1880s, the racetrack property was subdivided and the high fence around the place was razed. However, the oval ring of eucalyptus trees that once surrounded the track remains.

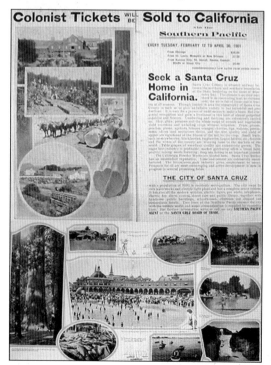

At left, a 1901 advertisement from the Southern Pacific Railroad Company urged readers to "Seek a Santa Cruz Home in California." The climate, topography, industry, and modern conveniences of Santa Cruz were such that "[i]t is easy for a person of small means to make a home, find congenial occupation, and gain a livelihood in this land of almost perpetual sunshine and flowers." At bottom, is a brochure featuring the second casino, redwoods, golfing, and other lures for 1920s visitors.

According to this advertisement, the "celebrated watering places" of Santa Cruz, Camp Capitola, and Aptos were easily reached by the Santa Cruz Railroad, connecting with the Central Pacific Railroads.

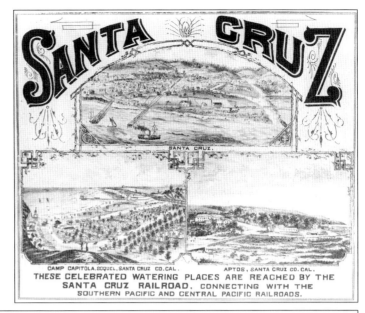

CAMP CAPITOLA, SOQUEL, SANTA CRUZ CO. CAL.   APTOS, SANTA CRUZ CO. CAL.

THESE CELEBRATED WATERING PLACES ARE REACHED BY THE
SANTA CRUZ RAILROAD. CONNECTING WITH THE
SOUTHERN PACIFIC AND CENTRAL PACIFIC RAILROADS.

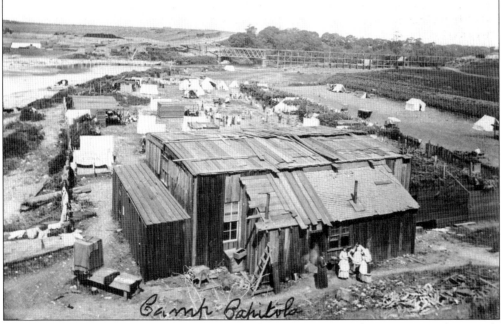

"See Capitola and Live!" This was it, in the early days. Promoters drew visitors to this seaside paradise with word pictures of its charms in the days before published pictures were common. "Located in a protected cove where Soquel creek pours its sparkling waters into the bay . . . the balmy atmosphere is rendered fresh and salubrious by the pleasant breezes from the bay," went one description. In the early 1870s, F.A. Hihn founded and developed the site purposefully as a destination spot for travelers wishing to experience nature and the fresh sea air. Camp Capitola's campground was north of the railroad trestle, where it was usual to bring or rent a canvas tent. Later cabins were square, pointed topped structures, available for rent by Hihn at a central office. Capitola succeeded and choice lots were offered on the bluffs above the beach, attracting wealthy vacationers who built homes that remain today.

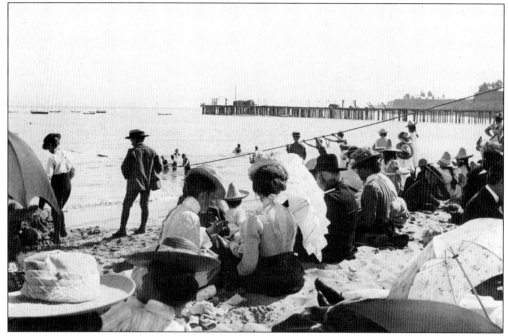

On Capitola Beach, c. 1890, shirtwaists, straw hats, and parasols were the beach fashions of the day. The Soquel Landing wharf in the background, formerly used for steamship transport of lumber and wheat since the 1850s, became a relic by the 1880s when shipments began to move by rail.

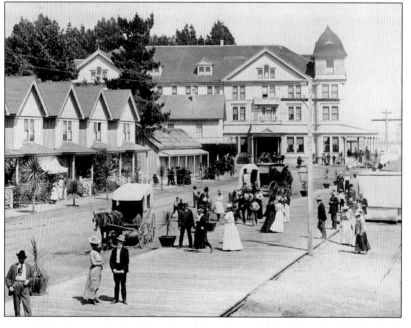

The beautiful Hotel Capitola (at the end of the street) was completed in 1895. It was completely destroyed by fire on December 16, 1929. The shake-roofed board and bat cottage (center) was one of the original Camp Capitola buildings. The row cottages (left), known today as the "six sisters," were still fairly new in this photo. They were relocated a block away in the 1920s; they still stand as popular vacation rentals. The Hotel Capitola was considered a first-class hotel. Capitola benefited by its designation as a rail destination, and photos of early streetcars are often seen draped in advertising for dances and other events there.

The 1895 Venetian Water Carnival was held on the San Lorenzo River in June. After the 1894 fire gutted downtown, the city fathers decided to hold a promotional event sponsored by millionaire James Philip Smith (whose stepdaughter, coincidentally, was chosen as the carnival queen). The river was dammed near its

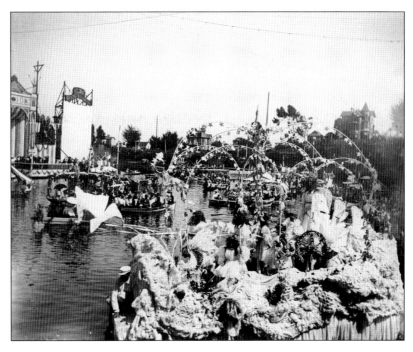

mouth, creating a lagoon, and bleachers were installed along the riverbank. Five days of events featured a regatta of decorated floral boats, music and entertainment on a river stage, "aquatic sports of the water olympics" (held a year before the return of the modern Olympics), velodrome cycling events, and strings of electric lights courtesy of Fred Swanton. Special excursion trains brought visitors to town for the event, which was widely covered by journalists including Ambrose Bierce and Frank Norris. The Water Carnival was repeated sporadically into the 1920s.

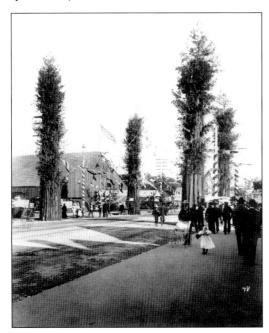

In 1914 the Venetian Water Carnival included several redwood reproductions, including one of a supposed pueblo stockade of the mid-1800s and the constructed redwood "trees" in this photo. Four pageant productions were offered on a specially-built river stage: "The Padres," "The Pathfinder," "Aladdin and the Lamp," and "Pageant of Peace." Post-1912 carnivals were staged on an island at the mouth of San Lorenzo called the "Opera Island" as a result. In 1914 the 100-foot island was landscaped to include a beach, "trees" (redwoods and a pine forest), and some buildings.

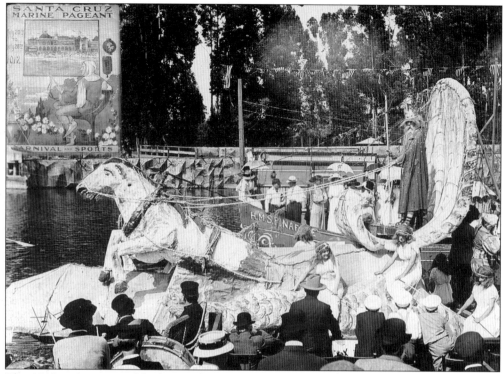

The 1912 water carnival had a "Midsummer Night's Dream" theme, but it also managed to work in the horse float seen at center, a Father Neptune character, and the usual fireworks. A hydroplane exhibition was held that year. Inset, top left: Water carnival program.

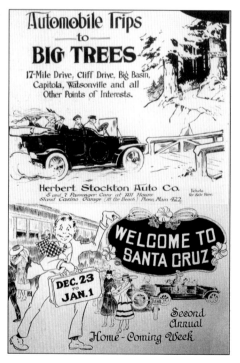

Automobile trips were publicized by postcards and advertisements. A common promotional device was the "motorlogue," a joint effort by auto dealers and newspaper publishers to promote Santa Cruz. Auto dealers would purchase advertising space in the newspapers, then send a news photographer on a scenic auto trip for the visuals. Right: Postcard advertising Homecoming week, 1916. As A.A. Taylor, owner of the *Santa Cruz Surf*, noted in 1915: "Automobiles, good roads, the entrance of women into public life, the growth of the prohibition sentiment, the movies, and other 'invisible' reasons have relegated the 'seaside resort' of the olden time to the scrap heap." This meant more tourists, shorter stays, and a boisterous middle-class beach culture.

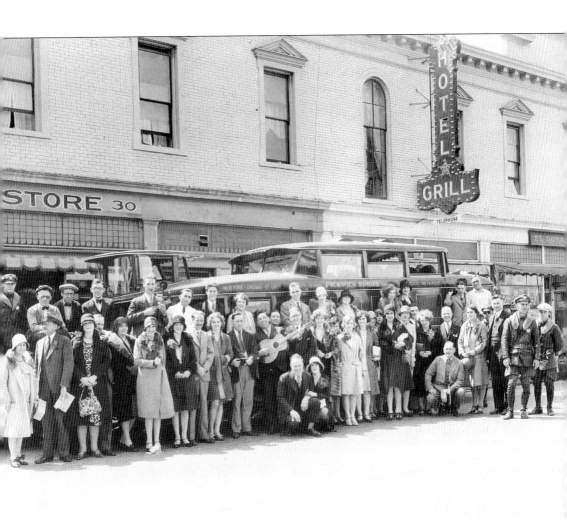

This is the Pickwick Stage Tour for the San Francisco Information Bureau, April 28, 1929. One day later, the Pickwick Stages company announced its intention to purchase Auto Stages Transit and Sierra Nevada Stages, two other auto stage companies that ran passengers from the central valley and western Nevada, respectively, to resort communities including Santa Cruz. The group is pictured on the west side of Pacific Avenue in front of the Curio Store.

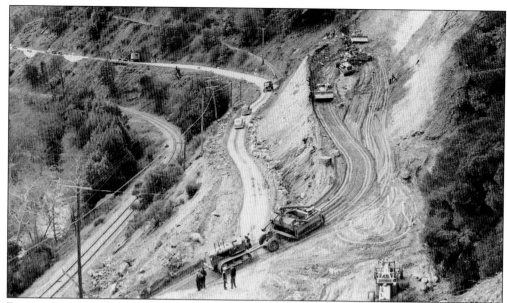

Engineering the Santa Cruz to Los Gatos Highway "required squeezing a highway in between the slopes of a steep hill and a railroad right-of-way at the base of it," according to the *Santa Cruz Sentinel*. The old Glenwood highway was already a problem in the 1920s when Santa Cruz's resort activities drew more and more automobile visitors; traffic backed up five miles or more. The construction of the modern highway began in 1931, was completed in 1940 and is today's Highway 17.

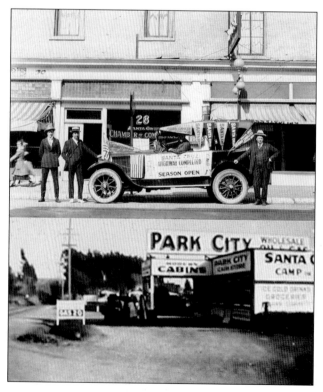

The *Santa Cruz Evening News* devoted a 1919 column to the need for more auto-related tourist facilities in the area. "Surely the events of the last few days must furnish proof of the need of municipal camping grounds for Santa Cruz. The hotels and lodging houses were utterly unable to handle the crowds of visitors. . . . If we want these people to come here we should supply suitable accommodations for them . . . we simply cannot afford to have people "pass up" this town." Top: The banner on the car reads, "Santa Cruz Highway Completed via Watsonville. Season Open." Bottom: Park City Car Cabins.

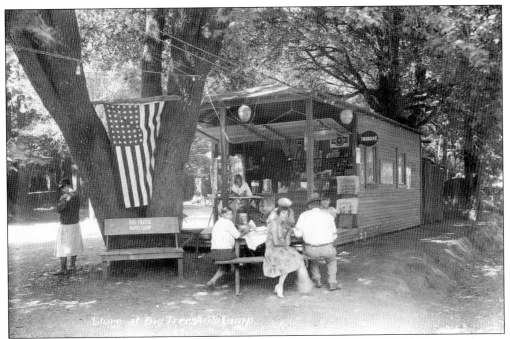

By the 1920s, tourists traveling by automobile required a new kind of accommodation. Forerunners of motels, called "auto camps," were rustic areas where visitors could park their cars and pitch tents. This family picnic took place at Big Trees Auto Camp, c. 1930s.

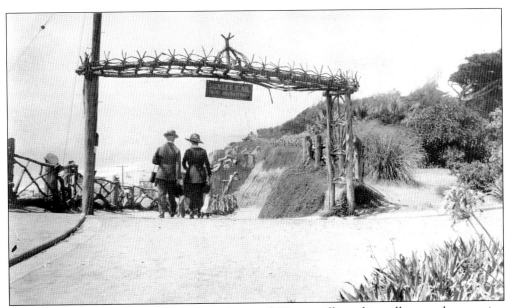

Sunset Beach is located between Santa Cruz and Watsonville and is still a popular camping place today. The sign reads, "Trail to Palisades Beach Road."

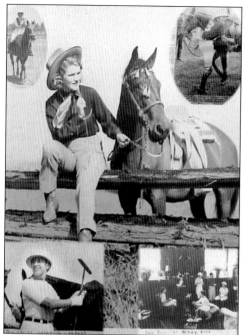

The Pogonip is a 614-acre site well-known to area hikers and nature lovers. Originally part of the Cowell Ranch, it was home to both a top scenic golf course and the polo grounds that housed the headquarters of the first United States Women's Polo Association. The property was leased in 1911 for the Casa del Rey Golf and Country Club. When competition from Marion Hollins' Pasatiempo course caused the Golf Club to close, the site was transformed into the Pogonip Social and Polo Club in the 1930s by polo champion Dorothy Deming Wheeler. It was one of the few polo clubs that was not restricted to men and that allowed coed games. The UCSC Library's Pogonip scrapbooks, compiled by Wheeler, document the heady early era of women in competitive sports. World War II ended the polo era at Pogonip, and the future of the site has remained unresolved for many years. Elaine McInerney, a local player, is pictured at center with her horse "Mae West."

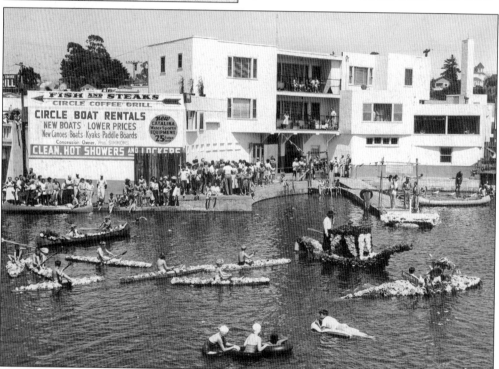

The Capitola Begonia Festival began in the early 1950s. It had its genesis in a water show designed by Peggy Matthews in 1950, which included swim races for boys and girls, an around-the-pier contest, a begonia-trimmed boat parade and a water ballet. By 1952 the begonia-decked floats were a permanent part of the water parade. Pictured is Capitola Lagoon at festival time, including appropriate advertisements.

Two photos of Axel Erlandson (1884–1964) and his "Tree Circus" on Scotts Valley Drive. Erlandson's 55 uniquely pruned and grafted trees became a tourist attraction in the 1940s. In 1963,

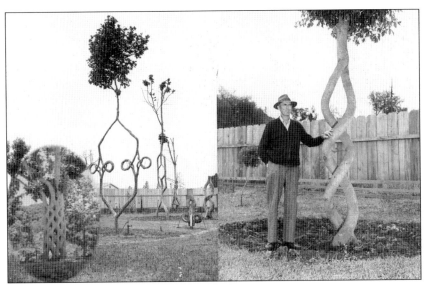

Erlandson sold the Tree Circus. It went through a period of decline, operating from 1967–1973 as the "Lost World" with the addition of large plastic dinosaurs. Architect Mark Primack "trespassed" to water and care for the trees in the '80s; his collection of material on the history of the Tree Circus is held at UCSC. The remaining trees were moved to the Bonfante Gardens in Gilroy in 1987. Nineteen of them have been rehabilitated and are a visitor attraction today. (Inset photo courtesy Nina Berry.)

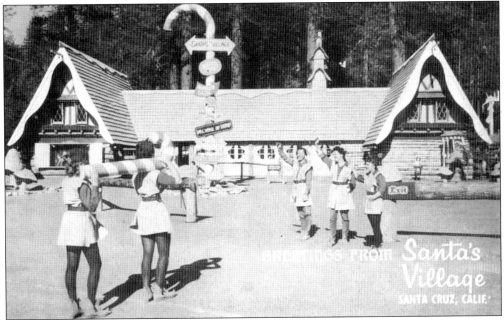

Santa's Village was a Scotts Valley attraction in the 1950s, '60s and '70s. Developer Glen Holland began building the theme park in 1955 on the west side of Carbonera Creek. It offered visitors 14 theme rides, 11 gabled log buildings, a petting zoo, and a toy factory. The park was also a wildlife reserve. Workers were dressed as elves, gnomes and storybook characters. Santa's Village Corporation went bankrupt in 1977 and the park closed.

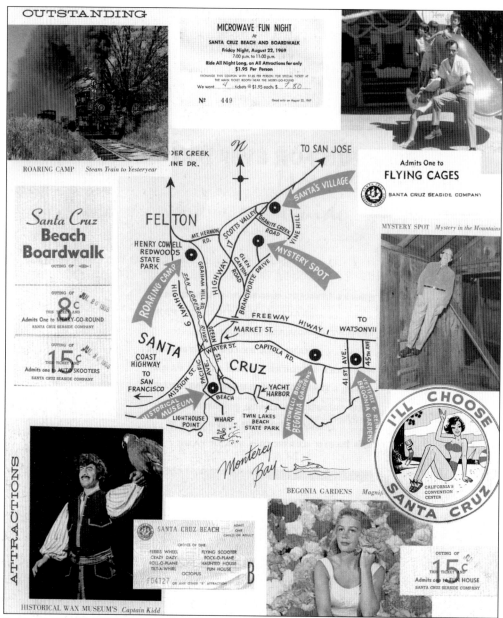

Santa Cruz had become a true day-tripper destination by the 1950s. Clockwise from top center: ticket to Microwave Fun Night, likely a group sales event for an early tech company; Santa's Village (courtesy of Annette Marines); the Flying Cages, a human-powered swinging ride at the Boardwalk; the Mystery Spot, first discovered in the 1930s, still hosting visitors today; ticket for Capitola's Begonia Gardens tour; MacDonald's Original Historical Wax Museum; Roaring Camp's "Steam Train to 1880," still operating as a tourist attraction today. Background: Santa Cruz Fun Map (courtesy Janet Young).

Seven
AN AIR OF PROSPERITY:
DOWNTOWN

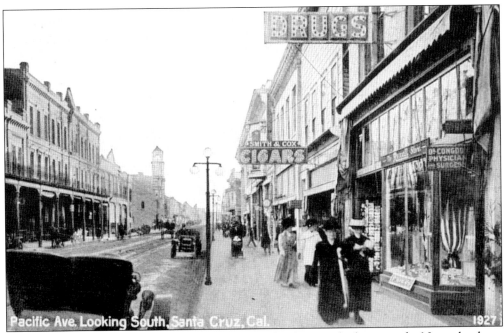

These downtown shoppers in 1927 are on Pacific Avenue looking south. Note the large gaslight at center.

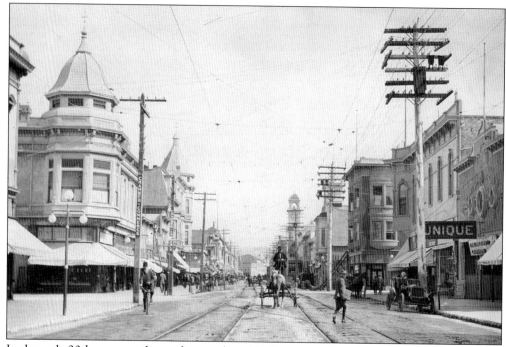

In the early 20th century, the roads were shared by horsecarts, bicycles, and automobiles, as this 1910 image attests. The view is Pacific Avenue at Lincoln Street; the Unique Theatre is visible at right. The buildings on each corner of the left side of the street, notable for their cupolas, were built by F.A. Hihn.

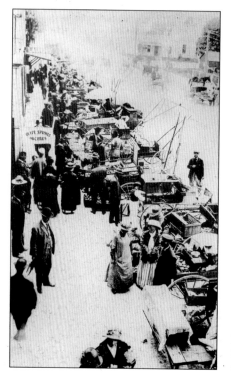

The Santa Cruz Free Market was in operation on Wednesdays and Fridays and drew numerous farm rigs (as many as 65 on at least one occasion) to a roughly two-block area along the east side of Front Street from Soquel Avenue south, c. 1910. Producer-to-consumer transactions involved fresh meat, fish and produce as well as jars of jelly and other home-processed goods. The farmers market downtown was revived after the Loma Prieta earthquake and is still a strong draw for the community.

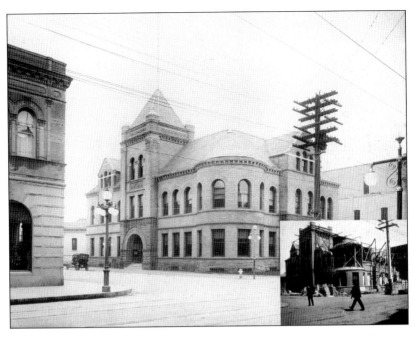

The County Courthouse (pictured above, *c.* 1915), later known as the Cooperhouse, was built in 1894 to replace the 1866 courthouse destroyed in the great downtown fire. On April 19, 1906, the 8.25 scale San Francisco earthquake struck; its radius included Oregon, Central Nevada, and areas south of Los Angeles. Inset, right: the County Courthouse during the post-quake rebuilding process lost its grand tower, which was never replaced. It was saved from modernization just in time to come back into fashion as the "Cooperhouse" of the 1970s downtown redevelopment era. It was a showcase for chic shops and restaurants and the center of a lively street scene. Sadly, it was the first to go after 1989's Loma Prieta earthquake. Though it appeared mostly undamaged, safety inspections revealed that damage from earlier quakes contributed to the structure's instability. A new, larger building on the site was designed to draw on the architectural design of the past, but for those who remember it, the old Cooperhouse/Courthouse remains the heart and soul of downtown.

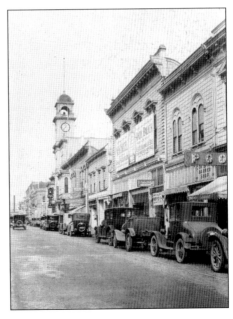

Parking was already a problem on Pacific Avenue, *c.* 1920. The view is looking north from near Walnut Avenue. Many will recognize the "Town Clock" shown here in its original location at the top of the 1873 IOOF building on Pacific Avenue. Business owners and residents of the downtown area were so unnerved by the chiming of the great clock that it was disassembled and remained in storage until 1976, when community donations raised the clock on a pedestal at the head of Pacific and Front Streets.

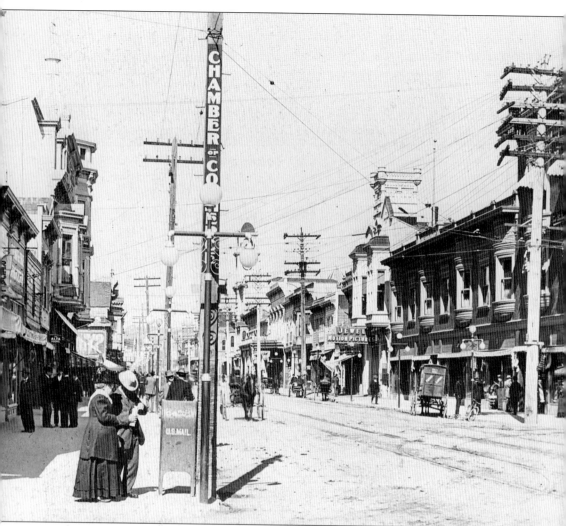

Pacific Avenue from the foot of Soquel Avenue was noteworthy for its mass of electric wiring: trolley, power and telephone lines competed for space, c. 1913. The wire wrapping on the utility pole next to the mailbox was there to prevent horses from gnawing on the pole. The "unsightly electric light poles" on Pacific Avenue were removed in 1922.

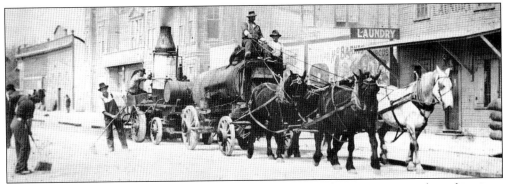

Local bitumen mines provided much of the natural asphalt paving material at this time, allowing Santa Cruz to enjoy paved streets earlier than other comparable communities. Cement began to replace bitumen at about the time of this photo, which was taken in 1916 at Front Street near the Naval Reserve Armory (building at center). City workmen are spreading hot oil and granite screenings; the steam boiler kept the oil hot and drove the pump that spread the oil from below. The driver is Jack Molares and the man at extreme left is Will McIntyre. Clarence Hynes (seated) is operating the boiler. At extreme right is Sun Fat Laundry, one of the last old-style hand laundries in the city.

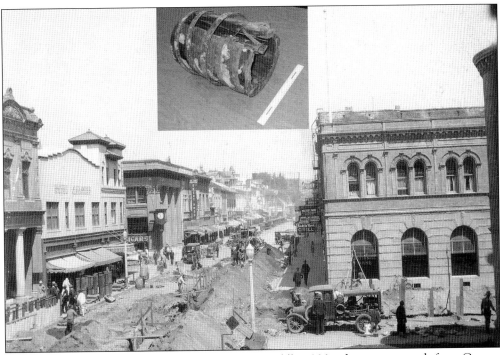

Pacific Avenue received a new sewer line in the middle 1920s; the view is north from Cooper Street to the Plaza. A section of redwood pipe (inset) was unearthed in 1991 from below Pacific Avenue when the downtown area began its redevelopment after the 1989 Loma Prieta earthquake. Landowner Elihu Anthony teamed up c. 1859 with brothers Hugo and F.A. Hihn to build a system and reservoir to bring water to Pacific Avenue (then Willow) by the use of hollowed-out redwood logs like this one. The old redwood line was found in the area of Pacific between Cathcart and Lincoln Streets. It was left in place except for this section, which was saved for posterity in 1991 by UCSC's Special Collections.

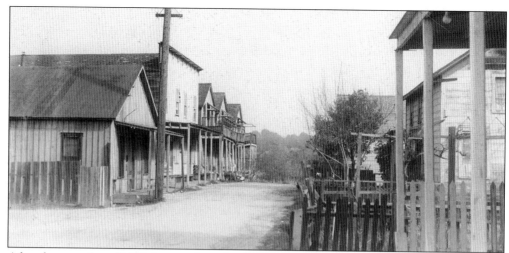

After the great fire of 1894 destroyed much of Santa Cruz's Front Street Chinatown, part of the Chinese population moved to George Birkenseer's buildings on Bellevue Place, an offshoot of Cooper Street near the river. This photograph shows approximately half of that Chinatown in the 1940s, looking toward the San Lorenzo River.

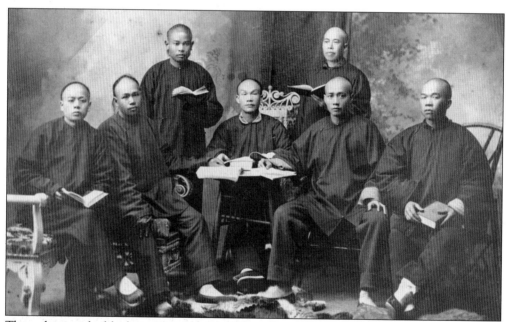

These distinguished-looking Chinese men with traditional queues, photographed c. 1900, were members of the Chinese Mission in Santa Cruz. The Chinese Mission was organized in the city in 1881. Adult members attended classes featuring English lessons and Bible study every weekday evening. The mission continued operations into the 20th century, but closed when the Chinese population in the area dwindled. Standing, at left: Chin Jim (?–1925) was an unmarried cook. Lem Sam (seated, center) was 38 years old and a resident of Santa Cruz for over 20 years when he was run over by a train on the railroad bridge of the San Lorenzo River in 1901. He worked as a servant and at times was a court interpreter. One of the first five Chinese persons baptized in Santa Cruz, he left a wife and an 11-year-old daughter. According to an indignant witness, the accident that ended his life could have been avoided if the train had slowed as circumstances required.

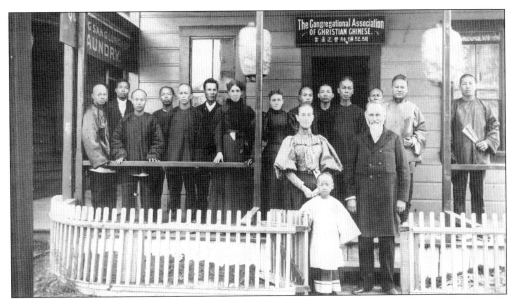

The Congregational Association of Christian Chinese, or Chinese Mission, was located next to a laundry (sign at left). Some of the people in this large group photographed in the early 1900s have been identified. In the front row, left to right, are Mary L. Perkins of Beach Hill, Ah Yum, and Reverend William H. Pond. In the back row, far left, is Chin Ong; fourth from left is On Chong (?–1921), a vegetable peddler who was born in Macao; second from right is Pon Fang (?–1924), who arrived in San Francisco from China at the age of 16 and was very active in the Santa Cruz congregation. He worked as a servant and later as a shopkeeper, and his daughters Ruth and Esther were "the only native born in the city [1909] and the girls attract much attention in their oriental clothing." Seventh from left is Kate Ingalls Hall (d. 1915), one of the very early graduates of the Santa Cruz High School. She was known as a devoted member of the Congregational church and a superintendent of the Chinese mission, where she taught for years. Eighth from left is Martha Ellis.

The Santa Cruz Chinese Free Masons Hall (Gee Kong Tong Joss House) was in decay at the time of this April 20, 1946 photo. An estimated 90 percent of the Chinese men in the city once belonged to this political and fraternal organization. Its patriotic purpose was to remove Manchu dynasty rule in China in favor of Chinese leadership. In 1930 the building was described by local historian Leon Rowland as an "old dilapidated structure . . . gradually going to ruin," and occupied by "three old men, looked after by the county, about the last of the old type of Chinese[.]"

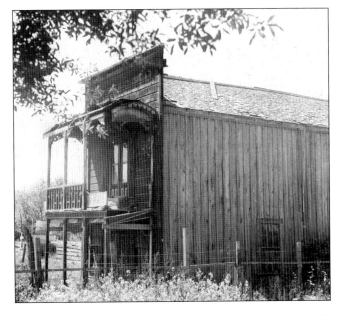

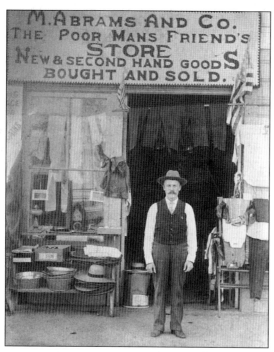

Morris Abrams, born in Russian Poland, arrived in Santa Cruz after a time as a traveling salesman and peddler in Los Angeles and San Francisco. His "Poor Man's Friend's Store" (pictured c. 1900) was located at the southwest corner of Pacific Avenue and Lincoln Street. He offered secondhand and discount goods initially, but gradually abandoned the "Poor Man's Friend" theme and became a successful vendor of a first class line of men's and women's clothes. The "Morris Abrams Store" lasted well into the Pacific Garden Mall era of the late 20th century.

Welcome to the "extraordinary junk establishment" of Wesley Fanning, amateur horticulturist, sewing machine repairman, Civil War veteran, chef, and philosopher; his shop was open 24 hours at 427 Pacific Avenue, according to a 1914 advertisement. Mr. Fanning was remembered in his obituary as "an odd old man, who lived in a odd old place and kept an odd old shop . . . but those who knew him better knew him as a man of much thought, vast reading, and an extended experience in many vocations." At his shop on

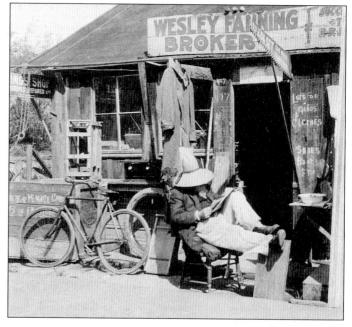

the corner of Pacific Avenue and Spruce Street, he bought and sold everything that was portable, "from hay rakes to watches, and also dealt in a philosophy of life peculiar to himself." Believing in the value of a strain of Burbank's spineless cactus as a forage plant, he cultivated a patch of it on the lot beside his store. He was also the owner of considerable property, including lots on Mission Street, agricultural acreage, and coastal view properties. His wife, May, was a spiritualistic medium and clairvoyant. By the terms of his will, his ashes were scattered over his cactus lot.

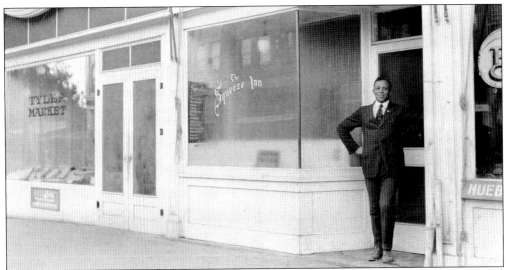

Louis F. Venable, one of Santa Cruz's African-American business owners, is pictured in front of his restaurant, the "Squeeze Inn," on December 31, 1919. The restaurant was located at 216 Pacific Avenue. It was particularly popular among high schoolers at the time. Venable sold the Squeeze Inn in 1920 and moved to Los Angeles to open a restaurant there. The new owners, formerly associated with a waffle shop, assured the public that the "Spanish dishes" served by the former management would be retained, even though eggs and waffles would be added to the menu.

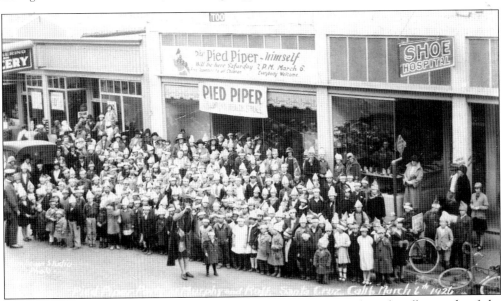

According to the *Santa Cruz Evening News*, on March 6, 1926, the sidewalk outside of the Murphy & Roff shoe store on Soquel Avenue was the scene of "a magic visit by the Pied Piper . . . the children were individually greeted by the picturesque musician of old Hamlin town and each given a brilliant hat and all had their picture taken. At two o'clock, led by the Pied Piper himself, the entire company of kiddies danced their way in a big parade up and down Pacific Avenue, thence back to Murphy & Roff's . . . where he told them the original old Pied Piper story and told them about the famous Pied Piper Health shoes which are wonderously made with neither nails or tacks and all about their healthy combination of flexible material."

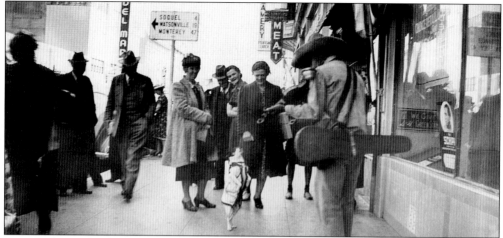

Downtown Santa Cruz has possessed a lively street culture for many years. This rare picture of a street musician and his dancing dog at Pacific Avenue and Soquel Avenue was taken c. 1930. Perennial street performers were often known by the tools of their trades; two relatively recent examples are Tom Noddy, "the Bubble Man," and Frank Lima, "the Accordion Guy." A statue on the 1500 block of Pacific Avenue depicts Tom Scribner (1899–1982) playing his musical saw; he was a logger and labor organizer as well as a performer.

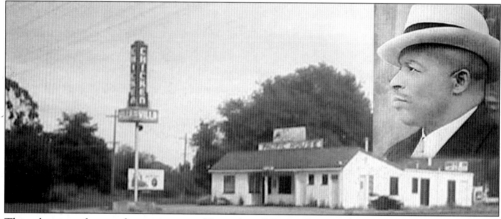

This place, at the southeast corner of Laurel and Front Streets, was originally known as the Father Divine Peace Restaurant, and was the project of followers of the charismatic religious leader. Father Divine (1880 ?–1965), born George Baker in Georgia, moved to the New York City area about 1915 and became one of the best-known religious leaders in America. His followers lived in communal-style housing and advocated the complete integration of the races and social activism (he once stated, "I would not give 5¢ for a God who could not help me here on the Earth."). During the Depression era, he had churches all over the country, and these "Peace Missions" (one was located at 21 Roberts Street in Santa Cruz) held interracial services during segregated times. The restaurant was opened in 1937 by Nancy Roussell, who took the name "Ann Sunlight" the following year. It was the target of some attention for the fact that its employees—of several races—worked side by side. Ann Sunlight herself became embroiled in a custody battle for her son that seemed to turn on the boy's contact with "dusky cultists." (The young man later received a good conduct medal for Army service overseas.) The restaurant was fondly remembered for good, cheap meals in hard times, and lasted until at least 1953 under the name "Chicken Villa."

In 1936, the Santa Cruz Chamber of Commerce decided to hold a public remodeling of an old building at the post office plaza. Similar projects were carried out in other northern California cities as part of an aggressive community modernization and building campaign under

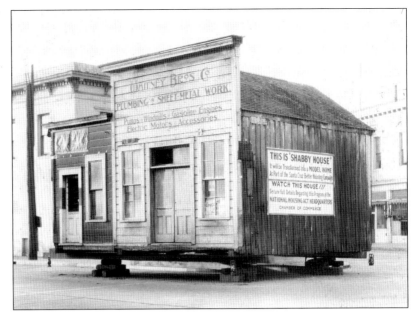

the sponsorship of the National Housing Act. "Shabby House" was kept open throughout its refurbishing to inspire similar construction projects and thereby revive the durable goods and jobs markets. The shack used in the project had stood on the east side of Front Street, where Whitney Brothers Plumbing had used it as a warehouse.

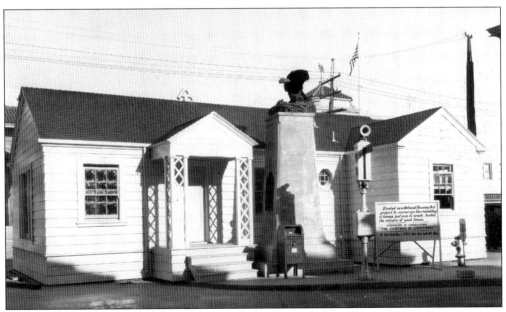

"Shabby House" in its new incarnation bore a sign that read: "Erected as a National Housing Act project to encourage the remodeling of homes, put men to work, hasten the return of good times. Information at Headquarters [of] The Chamber of Commerce. Do Your Part, Buy a Ticket, You May Win This House." Note the War Memorial statue in its "front yard," which fixes its location exactly at the head of Pacific, Front, and Soquel Avenues. It found its permanent home when it was moved up Mission Hill to Santa Cruz's west side and is there still, a family residence.

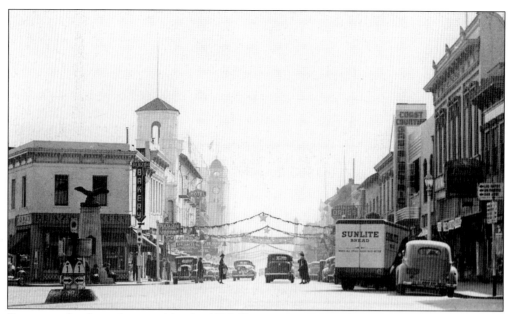

Downtown has been decorated for the 1939 Christmas season in this view at the head of Pacific and Front Streets. The statue in front of the flatiron building at left is a war memorial in honor of the "the soldiers and sailors of all wars" and lists the names of those young men and women killed in World War I. It was dedicated on May 30, 1928. This statue was recently reinstated in style after reconstruction of the site of the flatiron building, which was lost to the Loma Prieta earthquake of 1989.

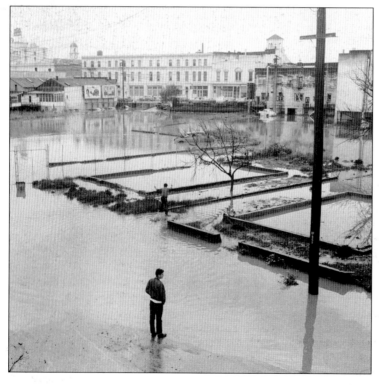

Downtown Santa Cruz looking west toward Front Street after the December 22, 1955 "Christmas Flood." The flood was not caused by a single storm, but was the result of a high tide, a river filled with wood debris, and a week-long gentle rain. It nonetheless left more than 400 acres underwater, including the downtown area. Pacific Avenue was temporarily uncrossable when the water surges reached a height of 10 feet. Pictured in foreground are Phillip Saldavia and Joe Saldavia.

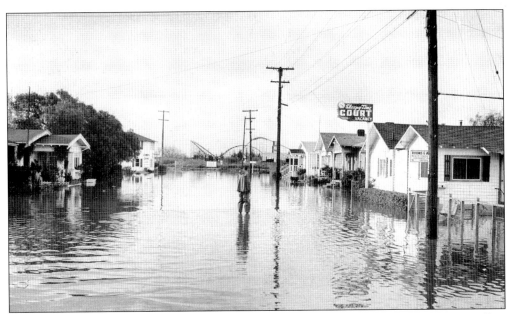

The rollercoaster is visible at the end of this washed-out section of Ocean Street near East Cliff Drive.

The full fury of the 1955 flood was evident at the picnic grounds at the mouth of the San Lorenzo River as it neared its outlet close to the Boardwalk. This photograph was taken at Beach and 3rd Streets. The damage left by the flood prompted drastic changes to the shape of Santa Cruz.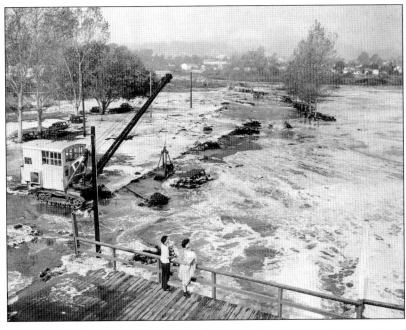

The Army Corps of Engineers replaced the riverbank forests with rock levees. Completed in 1959, the project was criticized for turning the river into a drainage ditch and for destroying the San Lorenzo as a fishing river. It also failed to remedy the flood problem, as it was so narrow that it could only prevent a flood one-third the size of the 1955 disaster. In 1982, Santa Cruz experienced yet another major flood that knocked out the bridge at Soquel Avenue. Downtown was largely spared, although areas in Rio Del Mar, Capitola, and San Lorenzo Valley were hard hit.

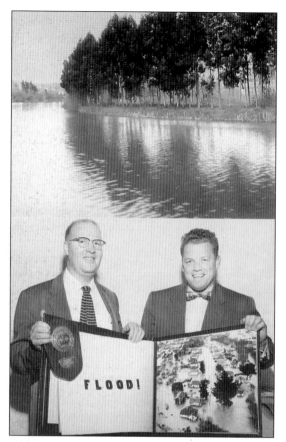

Pictured is a row of trees (top), looking upstream of the San Lorenzo River from the Laurel Street extension, showing the river as it once was in the downtown area. The Barson pear orchard is on the right. The entire area is gone now, part of the redevelopment area (today's San Lorenzo Street). Bottom: Why are these men smiling? Pictured are Oliver Aubrey and Bob Boucke of the Exchange Club. The devastating "Christmas Eve Flood" of 1955 was a genuine disaster, but with redevelopment came money. At a time when Santa Cruz had a "sleepy town" image, with little industry, only modest day-tripper tourism, and no university, community leaders couldn't help but think of the cash benefits of redevelopment. Sadly, the end result of the river development was what many view as a concrete lined ditch, while old buildings that appeal to today's sensibilities were razed and replaced. Some say the town was never the same after the flood, and that while the influx of cash brought some economic improvements, Santa Cruz forever lost a precious opportunity to capitalize on the river's beauty.

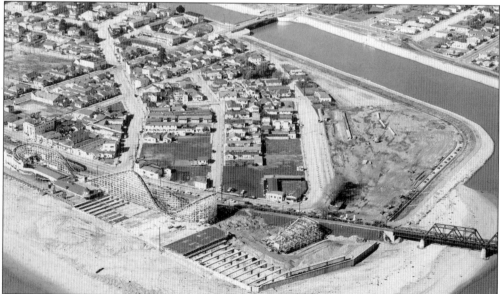

This is Santa Cruz Beach at the river mouth, five years after the deadly 1955 flood. The river has been confined and straightened, and the Boardwalk expanded. At the river bend, where once an island was home to spectacular water carnivals, a parking lot is under construction.

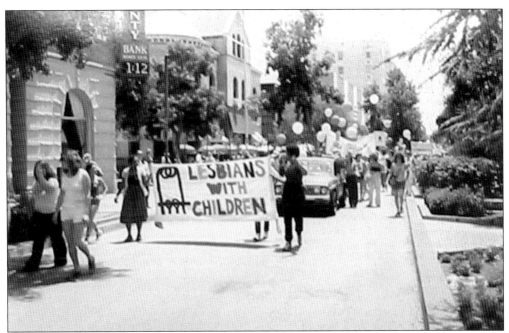

Unlike many other city centers, Santa Cruz's downtown survived the trend to relocate businesses to suburban areas, and even now it remains the focal point for community activities. Here we see some of the familiar 19th century landmarks: the old Courthouse/Cooperhouse is at center left, the Palomar Hotel in the distance, and the County Bank building, intact before the earthquake, is at front left. Pictured is a Gay Pride parade down the Pacific Garden Mall, 1981.

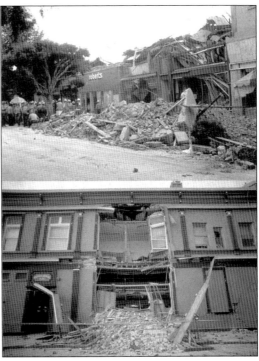

A magnitude 6.9 earthquake, centered near Loma Prieta peak in the Santa Cruz Mountains (nine miles northeast of Santa Cruz), occurred on October 17, 1989, at 5:04 p.m. Top: Rescue efforts at Pacific Garden Mall. (Photographer C.E. Meyer, U.S. Geological Survey.) Bottom: Many downtown buildings were damaged, including the outer wall of the Medico Dental Building, Pacific Garden Mall. (Photographer J.K. Nakata, U.S. Geological Survey.) Located on the fertile, if unstable, sandy soil of the San Lorenzo River bed, and typified by older 19th-century buildings of unreinforced brick, downtown damage was substantial. Six lives were lost locally, several in the downtown area.

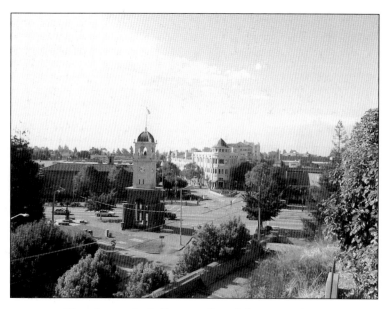

Although it has survived fire, flood, and several earthquakes, downtown is thriving today (2002). But it wasn't always so: after the 1955 flood, downtown Santa Cruz became a potential urban renewal project. Planners sought to shift traffic from downtown to freeway-linked corridors (from Pacific Avenue to Ocean Street) and to discourage mixed-use structures. The plan worked all too well, and downtown began to decline for the first time in the city's history. Thus in 1963 city planners proposed a total demolition of downtown buildings except for City Hall, the Octagon building and the post office, a drastic solution. Photographers Chuck and Esther Abbott, who came to Santa Cruz to retire in the same year, were instrumental in preserving downtown buildings from total destruction. Instead, thanks to their efforts (and not without controversy), downtown was reborn as the tree-lined "Pacific Garden Mall" in 1968 in hopes of capitalizing on a revival of interest in Victorian architecture. Today, even that heroic "save" is history after the ruinous Loma Prieta earthquake, and so the cycle begins again. This view shows the old IOOF clock tower, now at the head of the avenue and a gathering place. Visible beyond it is the new "flatiron building," built in the general spirit of its predecessor, and the St. George Hotel, a virtual duplicate of the old one. Many of the old brick buildings are gone, but the downtown is still the heart of Santa Cruz.

This 15-by-30-foot yellow and blue sign was installed in September 2001 at the corner of River Street and Highway 1. The "River Street Sign" was approved in 1996 as a means of drawing more attention to River Street businesses. Designed by the San Francisco architectural firm of Freedman, Tung, and Bottomly, the sign cost $83,000 to build. It was funded by federal and state transportation grants as part of the River Street improvement project, which included street widening and

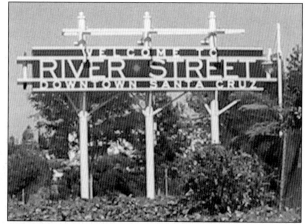

improved lighting. Public opinion toward the sign was favorable in its planning stage, but the completed version was variously characterized as "an atrocity" and an "unseemly entrance marker to the city." As of 2002, the controversial sign had twice failed to sell on eBay, but by 2004 it seems to be on its way to becoming an accepted local landmark. .

Eight
QUITE A DIFFERENT WORLD:
LIFE IN SANTA CRUZ COUNTY

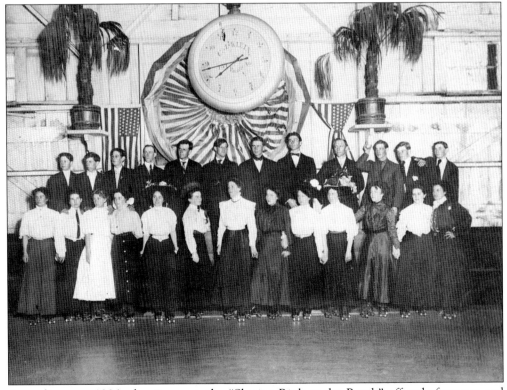

According to a 1906 advertisement, the "Skating Rink at the Beach" offered afternoon and evening fun accompanied by the Rink Brass Band.

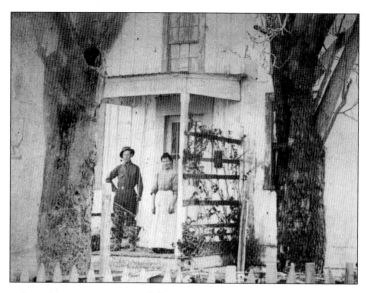

In 1916, this simple house was located facing Potrero Street at its intersection with River Street. Nonetheless, it had acquired its own lore in the city's life: an Indian was allegedly hanged in the upstairs (date unknown), and former residents named Stubendorff had operated a well-remembered shoe repair business in a back room of the house. The Farmer's Exchange had a building on the site after this house was torn down, and the Sash Mill occupies the location currently. On the porch are Louis Codiga and his mother, Carolyn (Mrs. Philip) Codiga. The Codigas were from Switzerland and immigrated to Santa Cruz in the 1800s.

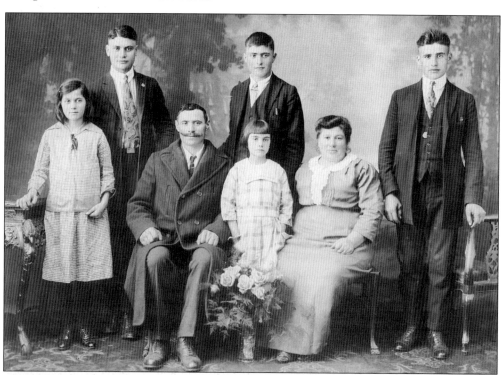

Whole families worked in the county logging industry; one example is the Anton Pesenti family of Boulder Creek, pictured in the early 1920s. Seated are Anton Pesenti and Anna Maria Locatelli Pesenti, his wife; standing between them is their daughter Michelina. Standing are (left to right) their children Conchetta ("Elsie"), Giuseppe ("Joseph"), Francesco ("Frank"), and Anton ("Tony").

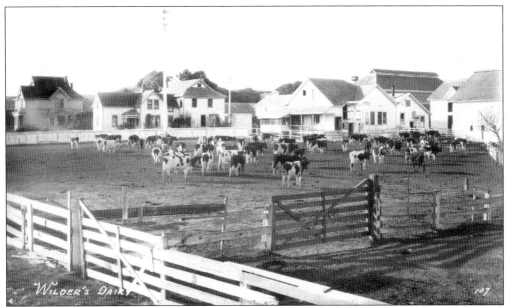

Wilder Ranch was well known in its day for fine butter and other dairy products. The ranch was an early innovator, trying new methods like installing electric lights so animals were awakened early. Legend has it that the addition of a touch of sugar ensured the popularity of Wilder Ranch butter in sophisticated San Francisco. With an address right on the old Coast Road a few miles north of the city, it was considered a premiere dairy operation, and it thrived. Later, new sanitation regulations required that the entire dairy operation take place under one roof, and the ranch was forced to retrench and replace its dairy herd with beef cattle. Revenues never recovered, and ultimately the site was purchased by a land development company; it was nearly turned into a large tract of residential housing. The property remained in limbo for years, but today it is one of the newest State Parks.

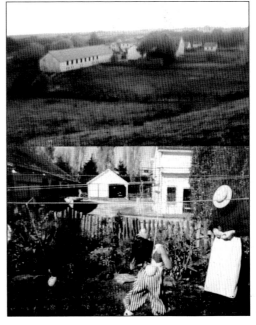

Wilder Ranch State Park offers living history demonstrations, tours of restored dairy buildings, and many miles of hiking trails. The building at top, pictured in 1991, is the cow barn, and the road just visible at far left is the old Coast Road. Pictured at the bottom are the games for children at the park, with Ranch staff member Nan Beltran. The blacksmith shop in the background was then under restoration.

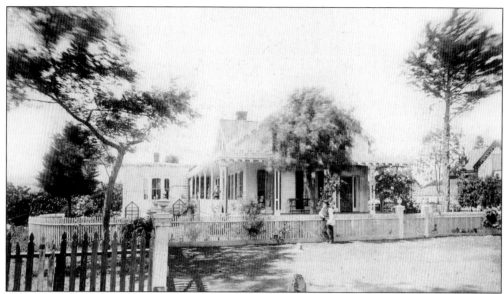

Around 1858, when Beach Hill was beginning to be built up, this residence was built on Third Street by Capt. J.J. Smith, a New Englander, who had a planing mill in the San Lorenzo Valley. He sold it to Mark A. Whittle, a lumberman (the man in the picture) in 1880. The house stood facing the north end of Main Street. Larger, more impressive homes like the Bowman and McLaughlin mansions soon replaced more modest Beach Hill homes like this one.

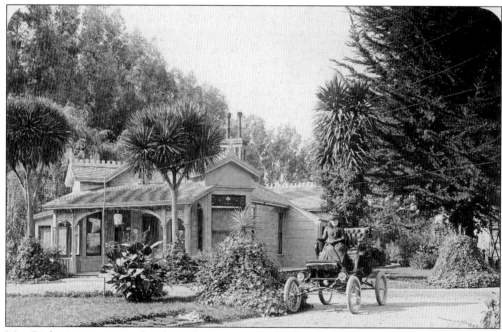

Mrs. Richmann is pictured in her white steamer at Phelan Park in 1900, on West Cliff Drive. In the 1890s, San Francisco mayor (and later U.S. Senator) James Duval Phelan used his Santa Cruz estate as a Bohemian retreat for guests including Jack London, Ambrose Bierce, Gertrude Atherton, and John Muir. Eastlake cottages and grazing deer were scattered throughout its wooded grounds. Most of the estate is now Lighthouse Field State Park.

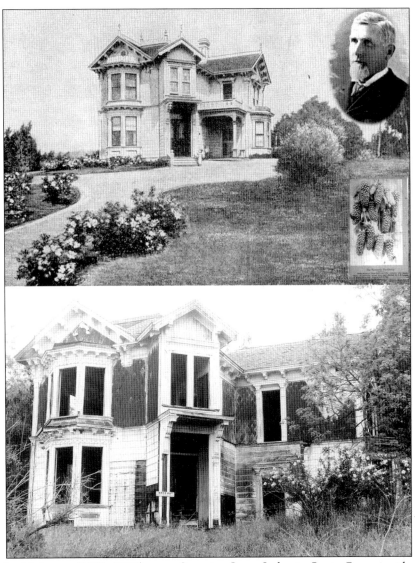

Judge John H. Logan (1843–1928) was a Superior Court Judge in Santa Cruz, president of the Santa Cruz County bank, and the founder of the resort town of Brookdale (a property he subdivided for summer homes). However, he is best remembered as a horticulturalist who began experimenting with breeding small fruits in his home garden at Santa Cruz. Judge Logan attempted to cross two varieties of blackberries and unwittingly planted them next to an old variety of red raspberry that had been cultivated for years in the area. The canes of all three fruited and flowered together and produced a plant that was similar to the blackberry parent variety, but much larger and stronger. This, of course, was the loganberry, a cross between the blackberry and raspberry. Top: Logan built this home in 1880, and it is where his garden was located. Made of redwood, the house was also notable for its sheet metal siding, which was painted and grooved to look like wooden boards. The house was located on High Street east of Highland Avenue, and had a panoramic view of Monterey Bay. Insets: Judge Logan and the loganberry, the latter at "natural size" (the berries measure between 2 and 2.5 inches in length in the original photo). Bottom: Sadly, in the 1940s, Logan's house had become the decaying shell in this photo and was razed.

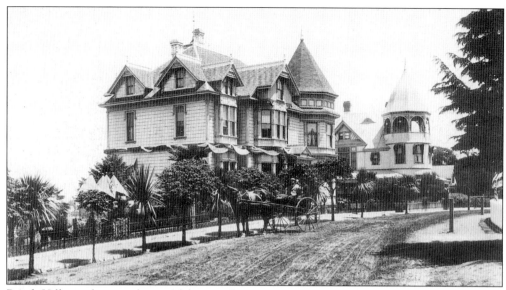

Beach Hill was the site of some of the grandest mansions of Santa Cruz. At front is the Gustave Bowman house, with Golden Gate Villa behind it. Bowman, a native of Ohio, was a successful hardware merchant and Santa Cruz mayor from 1882 to 1892. His 1880s mansion was torn down in 1936 by his daughter and son-in-law, Mr. and Mrs. H.R. Judah. The Judahs replaced the house with a Streamlined Moderne home (still located at 1012 3rd Street), described by architectural guide author John Chase as the "offspring of a toaster and an ocean liner."

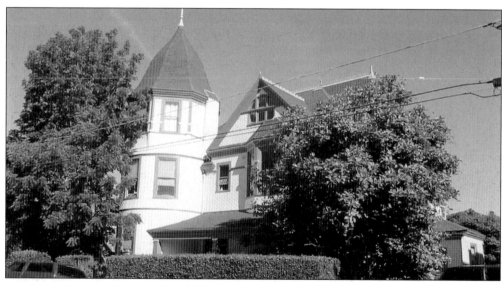

Golden Gate Villa still stands at 924 3rd Street. Built in 1892 by Maj. Frank McLaughlin, mining engineer and entrepreneur, it was also the scene of a family tragedy. In 1907, the widowed McLaughlin shot his stepdaughter Agnes and committed suicide by taking cyanide. The motivation for the act remains mysterious. McLaughlin had attempted an ambitious and expensive gold mining endeavor on the Feather River that failed miserably, but his estate contained enough money to satisfy his debts. His relationship with Agnes, then in her 30s, has also given rise to speculation. The house was later known as the Palais Monte Carlo, and was restored by Patricia Sambuck Wilkinson. It was listed for sale in 2002 at $8 million.

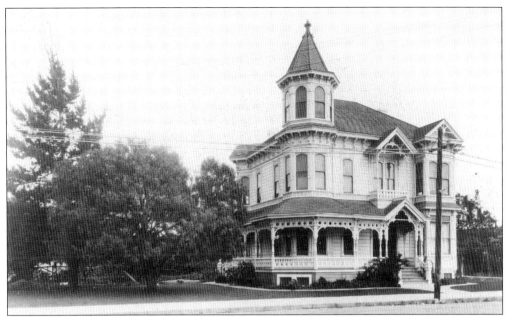

The Thomas J. Weeks house at 724 California Street was erected in 1886–88 for Weeks by contractor LeBaron Olive. Weeks came to California as a '49er, moved to Santa Cruz around 1850, and raised potatoes on leased land, benefiting from resale at high Gold Rush prices. He later owned a farm and orchard in Santa Cruz. It was known as a "hippie house" in the 1960s and '70s. Today it is a private residence.

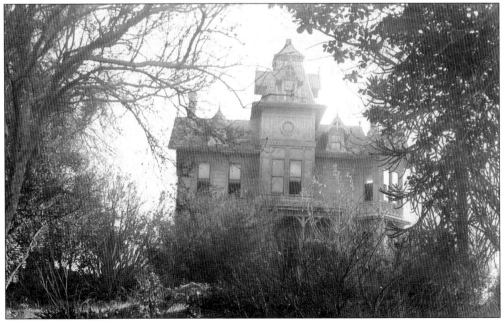

By the 1940s, houses like this one were "eyesores" and they could not survive redevelopment efforts. This house was built for Reuben Bernheim at Soquel Avenue and Riverside Avenue in 1883 by local architect J. Williams for $5,000. Razed in the 1940s, the house provided salvageable lumber, and its site was developed for commercial use (a drive-in hardware store).

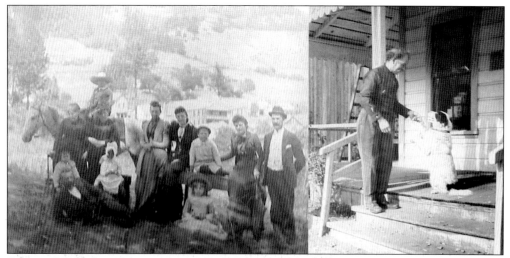

Felton officially became a town in 1868. Its heyday in the 1870s–1880s coincided with lumber transportation by flume and rail, and thereafter it became a quiet town. Pictured at left are three generations of the S.P. Hall family and their horse "Pedro" in Felton, c. 1892. The buildings in the background are the hotel and Frank Rodriguez's store; at right are Rodriguez and his dog "Jeff." Rodriguez's Felton store was located at the intersection of Highway 9 and Mt. Hermon Road. J. Frank Rodriguez (1848?–1935) was born in Monterey before the Gold Rush and came to Felton in the early lumber boom era. He was the town barber, storekeeper, and ice cream parlor operator. Jeff, who knew more than 50 tricks, was popular with visitors.

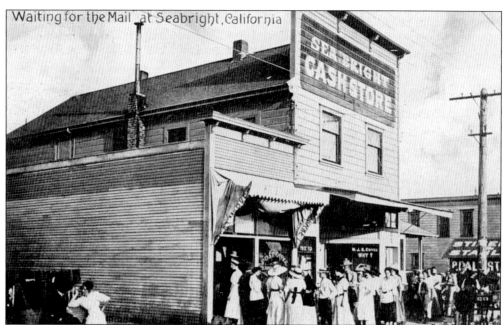

In the 1880s, Seabright developed as a seaside resort. Residents of San Francisco and Oakland purchased summer homes in the area. It had its own post office and station on the Southern Pacific Railroad line, and was not annexed to Santa Cruz until 1904. Pictured are residents "waiting for the mail." The post office was attached to a grocery store, so those in line for letters could also buy bread and groceries at the same window.

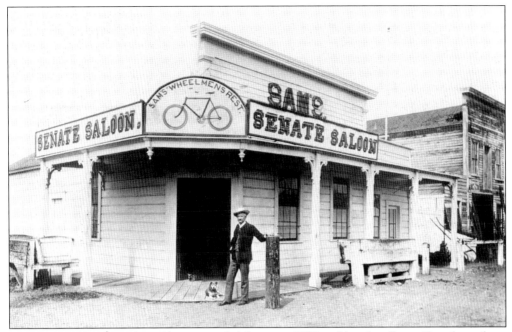

Samuel H. Alkire (1845–1930) came to California in 1853 and lived in Santa Cruz from about 1890 until his death. Pictured here in approximately 1900, his business was located in Soquel at the corner of Old San Jose Road. Bicycling was so popular in the 1880s and 1890s that cyclists formed the League of American Wheelman, now called the League of American Bicyclists, which lobbied for better roads. The Safety bicycle, introduced in 1885, looked much like today's bicycles, though the tires were solid rubber. Pneumatic tires only became common in the beginning of the 20th century. Today Santa Cruz is still rated highly for its availability of off-road bike trails and its attention to bicyclists' needs.

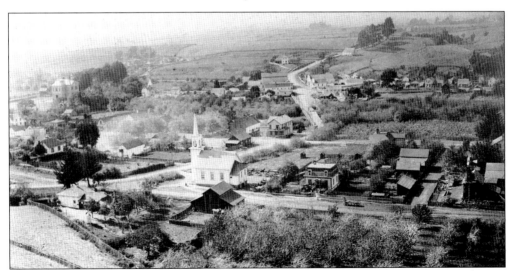

Soquel was established in the 1850s, but it never incorporated as a city. Its best-known landmark, seen in this early photo, is the Congregational Church on Soquel Avenue, sometimes called "the little white church in the vale." The church was built around 1870. Despite changes, this view is instantly recognizable today.

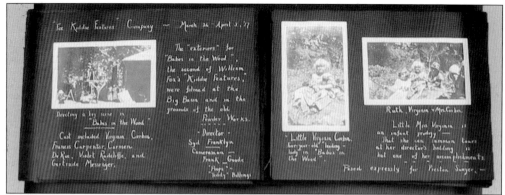

Young photographer Preston Sawyer compiled notebooks of "Movie Snaps" in the 1910s, featuring films made in Santa Cruz. Photos of film scenes, candid shots, and detailed annotations capture the freewheeling, "let's put on a show" quality of early silent filmmaking. *Babes in the Wood*, a 1917 silent film starring Virginia Corbin and produced by the Fox Film Company, made full use of a setting in the Santa Cruz redwoods. Ninety-two local children had roles as extras, mostly playing fairies and elves. The left-hand page notes in part: "March 26–April 3, '17. The "exteriors" for *Babes in the Wood*, the second of William Foxe's "Kiddie Features," were filmed at the Big Basin and in the grounds of the old Powder Works." On the right-hand page is "Little Virginia Corbin, four-year-old leading lady in *Babes in the Wood*. Ruth, Virginia, and Mrs. Corbin. Little Virginia is an infant prodigy—that she can summon tears at her director's bidding is but one of her accomplishments. Posed expressly for Preston Sawyer."

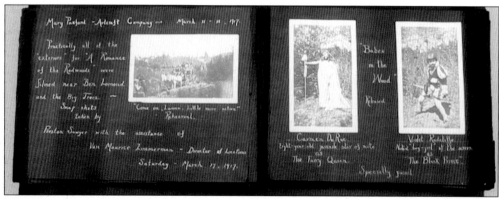

Santa Cruz County was a preferred location in the silent era, and many films were made there; Preston Sawyer's scrapbook documents visits from stars including Mary Pickford and Mary Miles Minter. Moviemaking was new then, and Preston was apparently given free reign to "snap" the stars at work. He kept careful, even reverent notes of every step of the process, and the autograph books that accompany the scrapbooks show that the visiting crews became quite fond of their full-time fan. The photographs show a relaxed cast and crew that didn't seem to mind visitors, as well as the speed with which they worked: several area films were made in rapid succession. Left-hand page: *Romance of the Redwoods*, starring Mary Pickford. Right-hand page: A *Babes in the Wood* rehearsal, featuring Carmen DeRue, "eight-year-old juvenile star of note as 'The Fairy Queen,'" and Violet Radcliffe, the "[n]oted 'boy-girl' of the screen as 'The Black Prince'."

Life was theater in early 20th century Santa Cruz. Top left: Joanna Wolff, the "Flag Lady," appeared in local parades in the 1920s and '30s. Top right: Jack Bradley, usher at the Unique Theatre. The Unique Theatre opened as a 700-seat vaudeville house in August 1904; it was later transformed into a movie theater and was demolished in 1936. To have been an usher at this time was to be "in movies"—a real job. Middle: Marcella Rostron (center), daughter of Rose Rostron, first woman supervisor of Santa Cruz County, and fellow dancers. Bottom left: Hazel Van Dyke (later Sivley), a local dancer, c. 1919. Bottom right: John Stockfleth of Garfield Street, a salesman who impersonated Abraham Lincoln in parades in the 1920s.

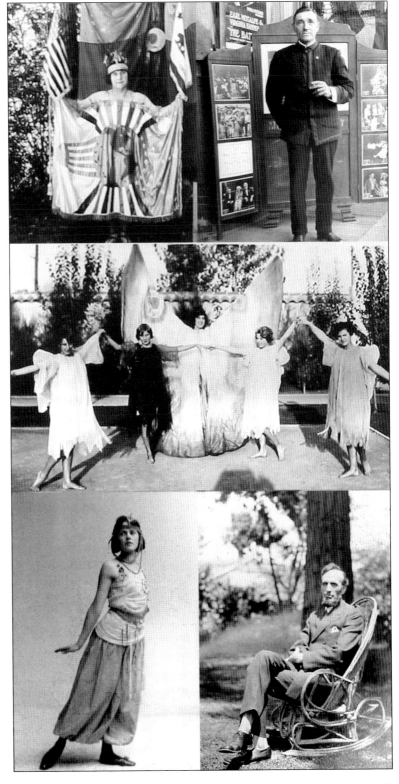

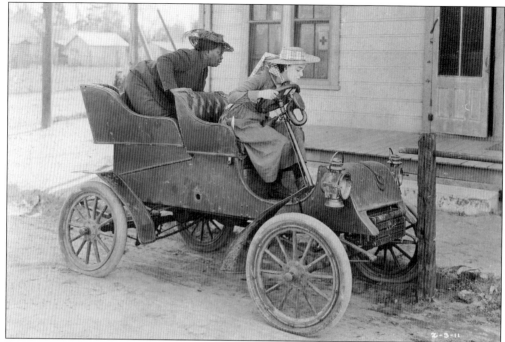

Zasu Pitts (1898–1963), movie comedienne in both the silent and sound eras, pictured here in a film still with an unidentified African-American actress. Pitts' family moved to Santa Cruz from Kansas in 1903, and she began her film career in 1917 after being discovered in a group of spectators while Mary Pickford was filming *Rebecca of Sunnybrook Farm* (Artcraft) on location in Northern California. Her downtown Santa Cruz home, located at 208 Lincoln Street, still stands.

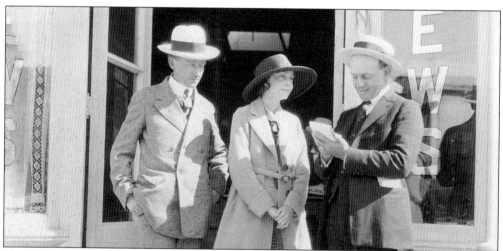

Zasu Pitts returned to Santa Cruz for a visit and was interviewed outside the office of the *Santa Cruz Evening News* in 1919. At left is E.J. Devlin; at right is H. Ray Judah. In the 1940s, Pitts was again linked with her home town when she purchased the recipe for the "World's First Candy Bar"—the Victoria Cream, a 1907 creation of Frazier Lewis of Capitola (the son of Patty Reed Lewis, a Donner Party survivor and resident of Santa Cruz). Pitts was an avid candy maker; she created the "Zasu Cream Bar," her version of the Victoria Cream that omitted the rum-soaked walnuts of the original.

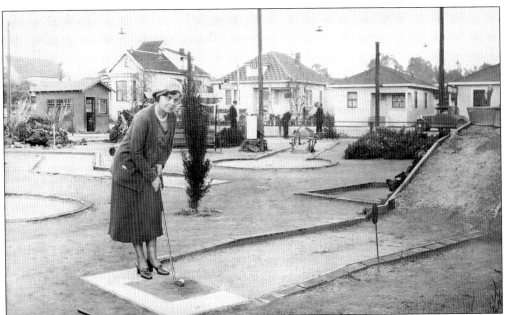

In the early 1900s, miniature golf was frequently called "Garden Golf" and it was played as a short regulation golf game with a putter on real grass. In the 1920s and '30s, "rails" or "bumpers" started to appear, confining the ball within a boundary, and the playing surface was changed to hard-pressed cottonseed hulls, which created a smoother putting surface. This miniature golf course was located on Ocean Street south of Broadway; the golfer is Gertrude Sawyer. The game fit nicely with Santa Cruz's resort appeal; it was a leisure game that any gender or age could play, and its scale allowed anyone to enjoy a sport that was once only played by the upper class.

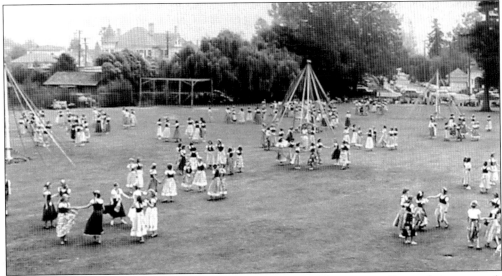

Maypole dances promoted both local dance studios and businesses. Pictured is one such celebration, held at the southeast corner of the Mission Hill School grounds. Some years boasted particularly extravagant May Day celebrations.

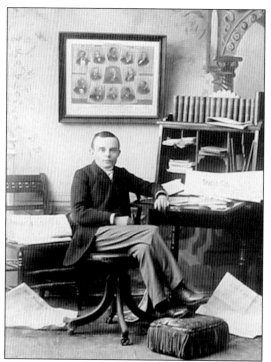

The writing style of A.A. Taylor, publisher-editor of the *Santa Cruz Surf* and mayor of the city in 1917–18, was strong on civic responsibility. His paper focused on exposing government scandals, one being mismanagement in the creation of the California Redwood Park (Big Basin) in 1907; he was a supporter of park creation and was appointed to its commission. He clashed often with Duncan McPherson, the owner-editor of the *Santa Cruz Sentinel*, which made for lively reading.

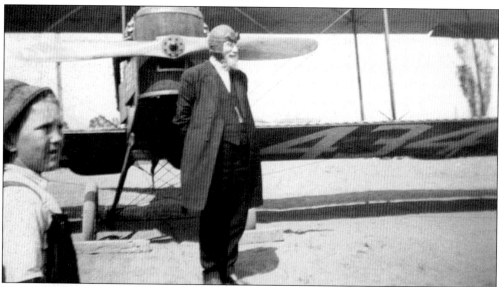

Duncan McPherson (1839–1958) came to California at age 13, moved to Santa Cruz in 1856, and worked in logging before becoming publisher of the *Santa Cruz Sentinel* in the early 1860s. McPherson was a respected editor, but history has not been kind to his promotion of anti-Chinese immigrant sentiments. The *Sentinel* itself proudly noted that at what was billed as an anti-Chinese meeting in 1882, "Mr. McPherson closed in a peroration in which he compared the Golden State of California to a second Eden, in which the Chinese were entering serpent-like, and from which either they or we must be driven, a sentiment which was loudly applauded." McPherson disagreed often with his rival A.A. Taylor, owner of the *Santa Cruz Surf*. The McPherson family owned and operated the *Sentinel* for more than 100 years.

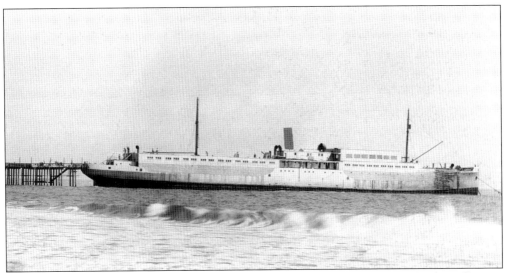

Called the "cement ship," the Palo Alto was built by the U.S. Government for $2 million in 1918–19 as part of a "concrete fleet" experiment when steel was scarce. The ship was towed to Seacliff and was later anchored to the bottom of the bay in 1930; a "floating amusement palace" was planned (tradition has it that the offshore location might let a little alcohol flow past Prohibition) but the timing was all wrong. The ballroom and restaurant opened just in time for the Depression. A heavy storm in 1932 ended the shipboard party forever when its hull was cracked irreparably. For many years the landmark hulk has been an interesting destination for fishing and bird watching. Community members have fought hard to keep it open, but time and weather have continued to break over it and today it is fenced off. It remains anchored at the end of its pier, as David Heron's book about it notes, "forever facing south."

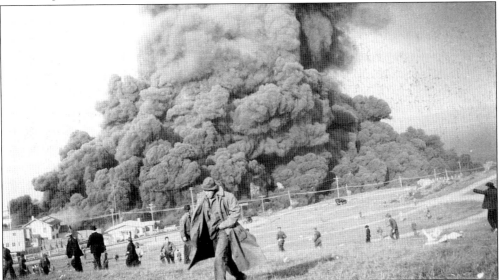

On June 7, 1924, a fire of unknown origin started at the Shell Oil Company plant in Watsonville. The contents of all the tanks went up in smoke. The gas explosions sent the flames up in the air, so the fire was relatively confined. Nevertheless, the *Santa Cruz Evening News* noted that "[t]he blaze was most spectacular." Other sources place this fire in Moss Landing at about the same time

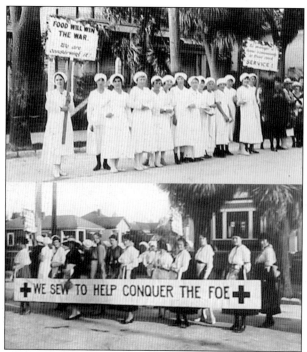

Santa Cruz women demonstrated their patriotism during World War I. At top, a group of women gathered on Laurel Street west of Pacific Avenue with "Food will win the War—We are conserving it" signs. At bottom, Red Cross workers at the corner of Chestnut and Lincoln Streets are pictured with their banner: "We sew to help conquer the foe."

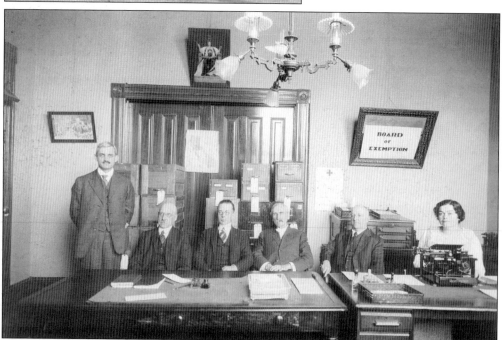

The Santa Cruz Draft Board (or Board of Exemption) in World War I was responsible for evaluating claims for exemption from military service. The Board was organized on July 4, 1917. Pictured, from left to right, are: Hubert C. Wyckoff of Watsonville, appeal agent; Samuel Leask Sr., secretary; Harry J. Bias (1879–1941); Col. William V. Lucas (1835–1921, resigned 1918 because of poor health); W.G. Radcliff (co-publisher, *Watsonville Pajaronian*), chairman; and Alice McIntyre, chief clerk.

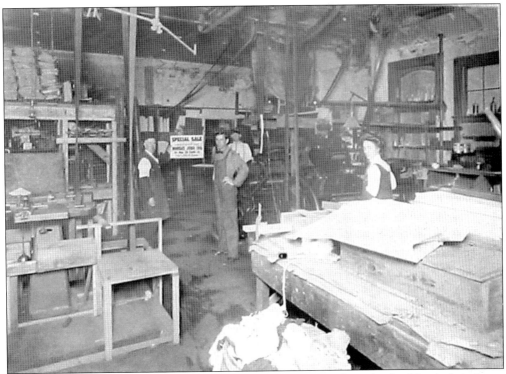

Newspapers have played a large part in the life of Santa Cruz, from the *Surf-Sentinel* rivalry to boosterism to day-to-day life in the city. This photo was taken in the pressroom of the *Sentinel*, located on Locust Street. Edith Fisher is the woman in the photo.

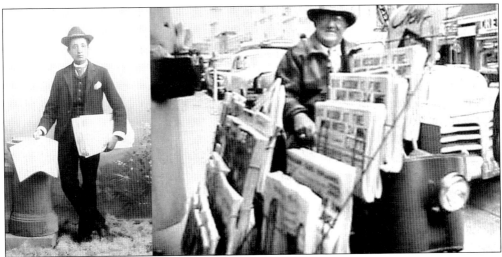

Newspaper sellers are always with us. Pictured at left is T. Garcia at age 17, with his newspapers on March 10, 1890. On the right is Harry Delameter, *c.* 1940, who sold periodicals from an electric chair on Pacific Avenue between Walnut and Lincoln Streets. He was crippled from the waist down from injuries in a lumbering accident and had the use of only one hand. Nonetheless, his success as an amateur fisherman was recognized in local papers.

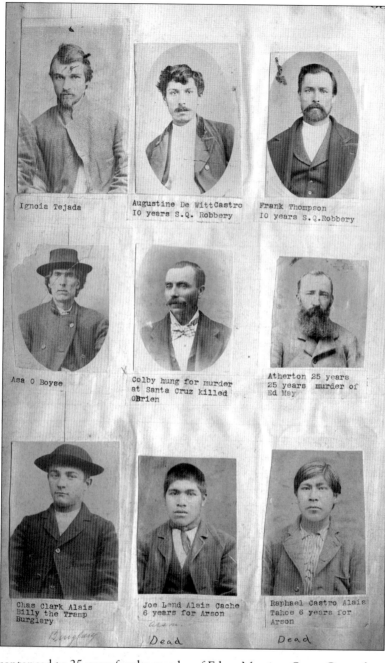

Ignoia Tejada

Augustine De WittCastro
IO years S.Q. Robbery

Frank Thompson
IO years S.Q.Robbery

Asa O Boyse

Colby hung for murder
at Santa Cruz killed
OBrien

Atherton 25 years
25 years murder of
Ed May

Chas Clark Alais
Billy the Tramp
Burglary

Burglary

Joe Lend Alais Cache
6 years for Arson

arson

Dead

Raphael Castro Alais
Tahoe 6 years for
Arson

Dead

One side of Santa Cruz was rarely depicted photographically. This page is from the Santa Cruz County Arrest Records, c. 1893. Pictured are, left to right: (top row) Ignacio Tejada, Augustine DeWitt Castro, and Frank Thompson; (middle row) Asa O. Boyse, (?) Colby, and M.H. Atherton; (bottom row) Chas Clark ("Billy the Tramp"), Joe Lend ("Cache"), and Raphael Castro ("Tahoe"). Thompson had been released from jail one day before he broke into E.P. Griffith's saloon and stole three bottles of champagne in 1893. As it was his second offense, he was sentenced to one year at San Quentin. Atherton was sentenced to 25 years for the murder of Edgar May in a Santa Cruz saloon brawl in 1873, but was pardoned in 1885; impassioned editorials attributed the reduced sentence to his prominent and moneyed San Francisco connections. Lend and Castro, two 19-year-old California Indian men, were found guilty of arson for an 1884 series of suspicious fires. The *Santa Cruz Sentinel* furiously attacked the pair as "bad Injuns" with no respect for civilized society. Neither received any legal representation, and both were sentenced to 6 years in San Quentin. Lend died there in 1886 of scrofula. In 1887, Castro was sent to the Stockton Insane Asylum, where he died one year later.

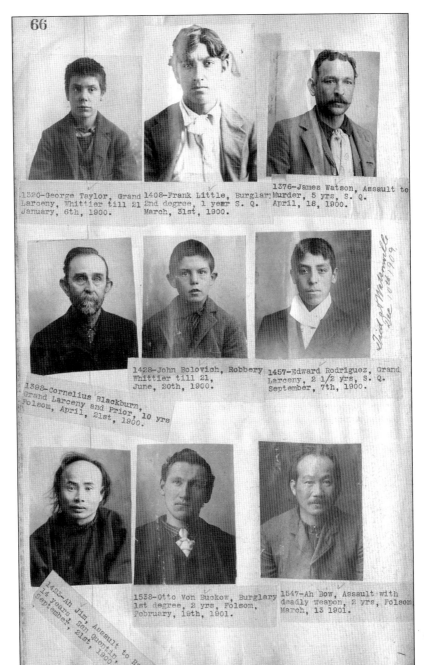

66

1320—George Taylor, Grand 1408—Frank Little, Burglary 1376—James Watson, Assault to
Larceny, Whittier till 21 2nd degree, 1 year S. Q. Murder, 5 yrs, S. Q.
January, 6th, 1900. March, 31st, 1900. April, 18, 1900.

1428—John Bolovich, Robbery 1457—Edward Rodriguez, Grand
Whittier till 21, Larceny, 2 1/2 yrs, S. Q.
June, 20th, 1900. September, 7th, 1900.

1398—Cornelius Blackburn, Grand Larceny and Prior, 10 yrs Folsom, April, 21st, 1900.

Died at Watsonville Dec 10th 1909.

1425—Ah Jim, Assault to Rape 14 years, San Quentin, September, 21st, 1900.

1538—Otto Von Buckow, Burglary 1547—Ah Bow, Assault with
1st degree, 2 yrs, Folsom, deadly weapon, 2 yrs, Folsom
February, 19th, 1901. March, 13 1901.

This page from the Santa Cruz County Arrest Records dates from the year 1900. Pictured, left to right, are: (top row) George Taylor, Frank Little, and James Watson; (middle row) Cornelius Blackburn, John Bolovich, and Edward Rodriguez; (bottom row) Ah Jim, Otto von Buckow, and Ah Bow. Taylor and Bolovich were juveniles. Blackburn was sentenced to 10 years for grand larceny for stealing a horse and buggy, as he had a prior murder conviction. He unsuccessfully feigned insanity at his trial, being labeled instead "the biggest faker that ever struck a court." (*Santa Cruz Surf*) Ah Jim was found guilty of the rape of an 11-year-old girl. Ah Bow, a ranch cook, committed suicide by gunshot in 1906 in the face of worsening illness and possible hospitalization.

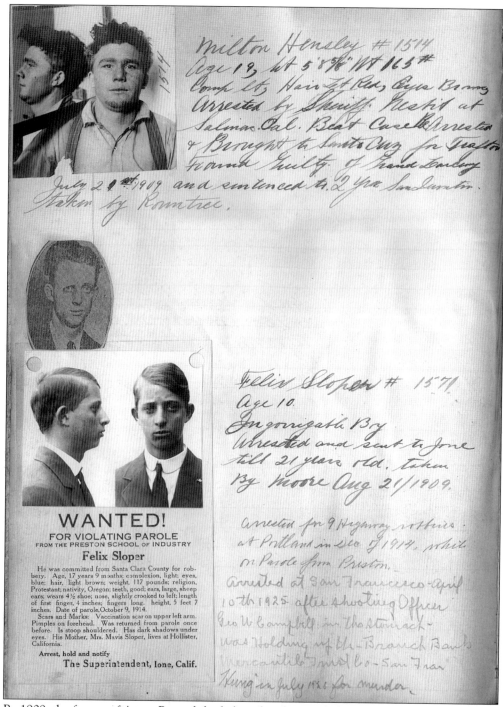

By 1909, the format of Arrest Records had altered and expanded. Pictured are Milton Hensley, top, and Felix Sloper, bottom. Sloper's entire criminal career—from incorrigible boy at age 10 to executed murderer in 1926—is set out on this page. The "Wanted" card with his description would have been sent to law enforcement offices. Hensley was photographed while holding a mirror, an effective way to depict profile and full face simultaneously.

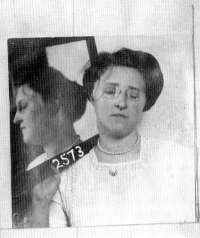

Tillie Duncan   2573
            alias Mrs. J.B.Edwards
Arrested at Watsonville with Frank Babbitt
on charge on Passing Fict Checks. Plead
guilty to charge ng was granted 3 yrs
Probation by Judge Smith. Released
June 6th 1913.
      Age 20 - Ht 5-ft 5 in (shoes off) wright
174- Complexion light. Hair Lt Brown. Eyes
Lt Brown. Mol front neck center. Left
Eye is crossed, Wears glasses.

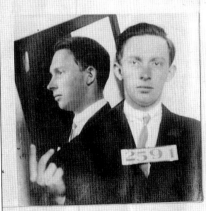

John H. Elmann   2591
      Arrested in Seattle, Wash. on charge
of Passing Fict Check. Plead guilty to
charge, sentenced to (1 year) San Quentin
by Judge Smith. Age 29 - Occupation
electrician, Ht 6 ft-15/8 in - Wt 172-
Complexion Light - Hair red - Eyes
Brown. Stands erect - Dished nose.
Taken to San Quentin June 5 - 1913
By R.H Rowntree San Quentin # 26579

Arrest Records from 1913 included images of Tillie Duncan, top, and John H. Elmann, bottom. Duncan, aged 20, charged with passing fictitious checks totaling $100, told her life story to the *Santa Cruz Surf* on June 7, 1913. She was encouraged to pass the checks by a man named Frank Bobbitt or Babbitt, with whom she cohabited. Given "her people, her youth, and her misfortune," she was released on probation, but first received a "strong talk" from the Judge. Elmann, below, was not so fortunate—his bad check offense brought him one year in San Quentin.

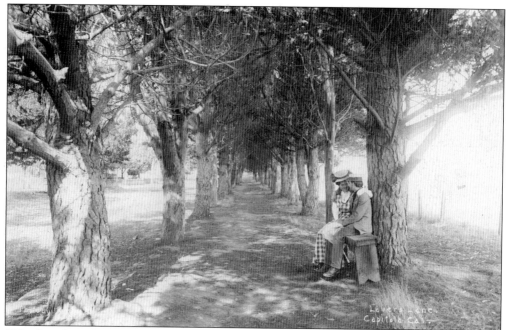

"Winding through the redwoods and ferns to Aptos is the prettiest of romantic woodland paths called, of course, 'Lover's Walk.'"(*Santa Cruz Daily Surf*, 1891.)

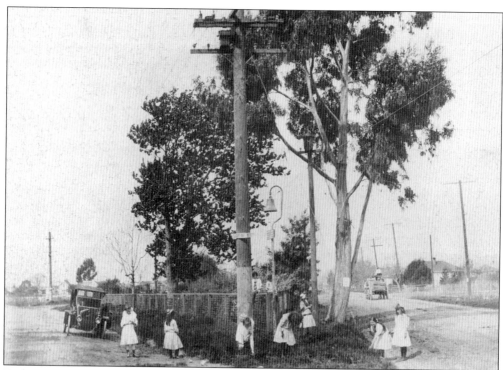

Today it is the busy confluence of three major crosstown routes, but the small triangle of land at the center was once "Triangle Park." Left is Soquel Avenue and right is Water Street; behind the camera to the right is Morrissey Boulevard.

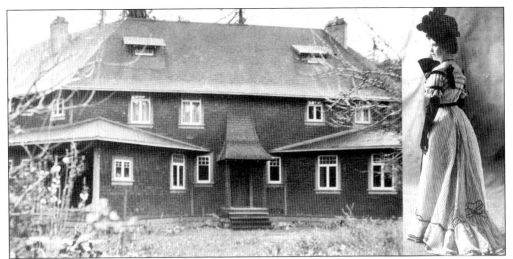

Hallie Hyde Irwin lived in Brookdale from 1904 until her death in 1962. A native of Oakland, the high style photo at right was taken when she lived in San Francisco, c. 1900. Her 1901 marriage to newspaperman and writer Will Irwin ended in divorce. She then married Will's younger brother Herman. At left, the Irwins' house in Brookdale in 1925. It was designed by Hallie and built over a 10-year period out of timbers, hardwood flooring, doors, plumbing, and other materials shipped from wreckers of the 1915 Pan-Pacific Exposition held in San Francisco.

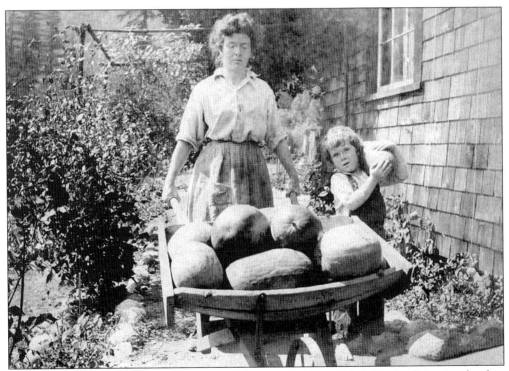

Labor, not leisure: Hallie Hyde Irwin and her son, William Hyde Irwin, bring in the first watermelon crop of the season in a homemade wheelbarrow. This photo was taken before 1910 in Brookdale.

109

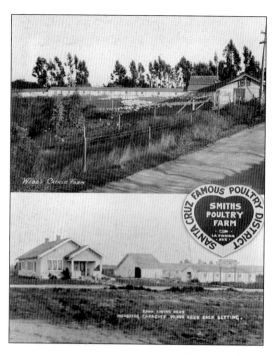
Webb's Cackle Farm

SANTA CRUZ FAMOUS POULTRY DISTRICT
SMITHS POULTRY FARM
LA FONDA AVE

Chicken ranching was widespread in Santa Cruz, but the greatest concentration was along the DeLaveaga foothills in today's Prospect Heights and into Live Oak, once known as "Chickentown." Street names like "Chanticleer" are a reflection of the area's past. At top is pictured Webb's Cackle Farm; at the bottom, Smith's Poultry Farm, "located in Santa Cruz's Famous Poultry District." One hatchery is still left in the Live Oak area, on Rodriguez Street.

Two years equaled 2,502 eggs! Egg laying was serious business in Santa Cruz in the 1920s, gaining national attention. Pathé news cameras were present to record the awards ceremony for the 1924 Santa Cruz Farm Bureau Egg Laying Contest, which hosted

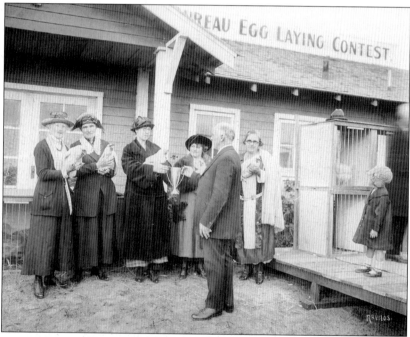

entries from throughout the west and Hawaii and east to Michigan and Florida. Here C.D. Hinkle, president of the Santa Cruz Chamber of Commerce, is presenting an award to representatives of the St. Johns Poultry Farm, Oronogo, Missouri, whose hens laid a total of 2,502 eggs in two years—a world's record. Also accepting awards that day were chicken ranchers W.J. Kenna and F.L. Collins, both of Santa Cruz. The names of the hardworking chickens were not noted.

This woman, photographed in 1919, appears to be assembling apple boxes. The first big apple orchard in Santa Cruz was located on the site of today's Pacific Avenue in 1856, on the fertile river floodplain; around the same time, apple trees were also planted in the Pajaro Valley. Apple boxes were nailed together on a form, with some workers bragging of assembling 120 boxes per hour. Felton Box Factory and the Santa Cruz Canning Company shared management for a time; in 1919 the box factory had a capacity of 8,000 boxes per day. Santa Cruz Fruit Cannery, Mountain View fruit packers, the tuna industry in the Hawaiian Islands, and miscellaneous other clients were on its roster. An item of trivia: the enormous success of apple growing in the county resulted in the installation of (allegedly) "the largest box making machine in the world" in Pajaro Valley in 1914.

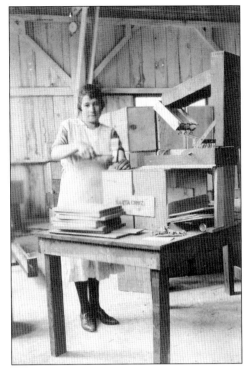

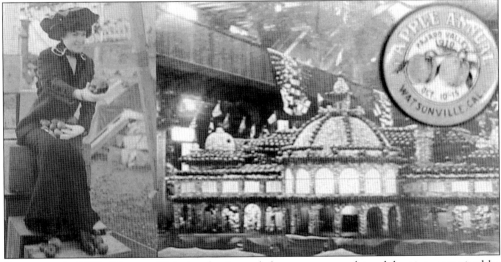

Beginning in 1909, Watsonville's Apple Annual show was a popular celebration organized by growers to celebrate booming sales and the growth of the community. In 1901, fewer than 200,000 trees grew on about 1,800 acres in the Pajaro Valley; by the end of the decade, one million trees filled about 14,000 acres. Watsonville architect William Weeks designed the neoclassical Apple Annual Hall on Second Street between Rodriguez and Walker streets; its stage was one of the largest on the coast. Creative displays (like this apple "casino") accompanied exhibitions of insecticides, sprayers, machinery, and apple-related products like cider, vinegar, and dried fruit. Competitions in box making, apple packing, and horse racing were held. The Apple Annuals ended with World War I, but Watsonville remained a center for food packaging and processing, culminating in significant labor battles in the 1980s.

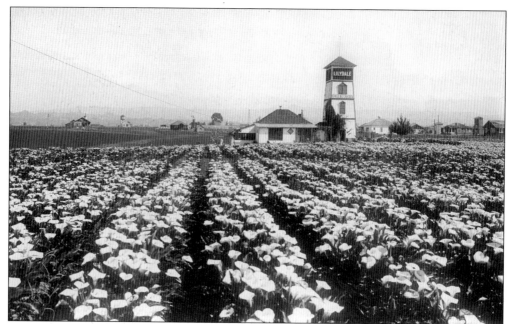

A few years after Colin H. and Sidona V.J. McIsaac came from Portland, Oregon, to Santa Cruz, they established a fine home above the Del Mar beach at about 17th Avenue. Flower fanciers, they opened Lilydale in 1909 as a bulb ranch for calla lilies and ginseng. The Union Traction electric streetcar line ran right by this point, and beginning in early spring, passengers were treated to this view of its extensive fields.

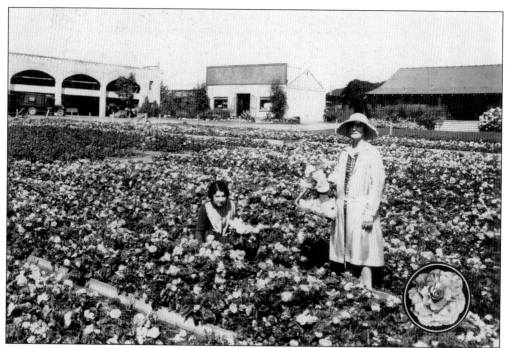

The H.A. Hyde nursery in Watsonville, pictured here in the late 1920s, produced tuberous begonias on a large scale. Mona Minto (later Durden) is at right.

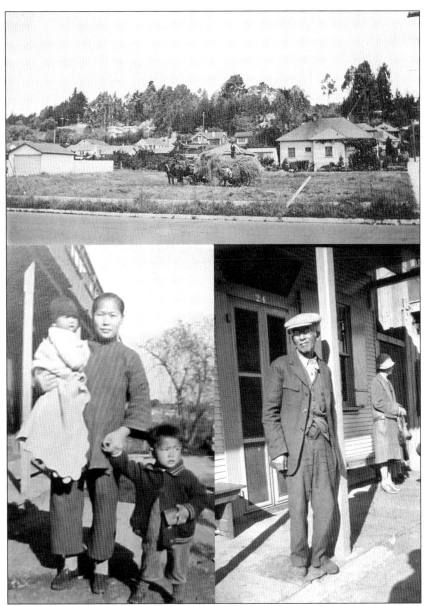

L. Alice Halsey—"Miss Halsey"—was a schoolteacher whose Italianate Victorian home across from the Mission Park still stands on a busy corridor of Mission Street as it heads to downtown. A hobbyist photographer, she owned a Brownie camera, which she used to document the ordinary life of her family, her neighborhood, and her workplace (Mission Hill School) throughout 1930 and 1931. Some of her subjects were casual, even candid: the workmen building the new school, haymaking along King Street (pictured at top), schoolchildren waiting for the morning bus, neighbors and local people downtown (bottom). But she also caught a daredevil "aerialist" performing atop the Palomar Hotel, nuns walking near Holy Cross Church, parades, tourists, and busy Pacific Avenue at mid-day. Fortunately for us, she was a meticulous note-taker, and carefully annotated the envelope for the each negative of every photograph she took. Most of the negatives in her collection, now at UCSC, have not yet been printed; these are a few of the exceptions.

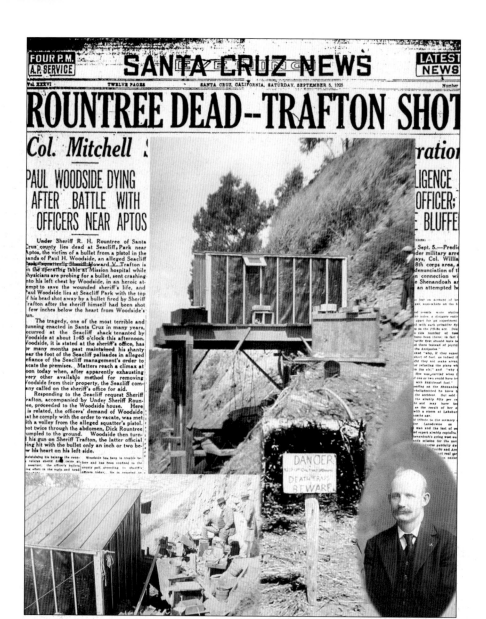

FOUR P.M.
A.P. SERVICE

SANTA CRUZ NEWS

LATEST
NEWS

Vol XXXVI   TWELVE PAGES   SANTA CRUZ, CALIFORNIA, SATURDAY, SEPTEMBER 5, 1925   Number

ROUNTREE DEAD--TRAFTON SHOT

Col. Mitchell

ration

LIGENCE
OFFICER;
BLUFFE

PAUL WOODSIDE DYING
AFTER BATTLE WITH
OFFICERS NEAR APTOS

Under Sheriff R. H. Rountree of Santa Cruz county lies dead at Seacliff Park near Aptos, the victim of a bullet from a pistol in the hands of Paul H. Woodside, an alleged Seacliff squatter. Sheriff Howard V. Trafton is in the operating table at Mission hospital while physicians are probing for a bullet, sent crashing into his left chest by Woodside, in an heroic attempt to save the wounded sheriff's life, and Paul Woodside lies at Seacliff Park with the top of his head shot away by a bullet fired by Sheriff Trafton after the sheriff himself had been shot few inches below the heart from Woodside's gun.

The tragedy, one of the most terrible and stunning enacted in Santa Cruz in many years, occurred at the Seacliff shack tenanted by Woodside at about 1:45 o'clock this afternoon. Woodside, it is stated at the sheriff's office, has for many months past maintained his shanty near the foot of the Seacliff palisades in alleged defiance of the Seacliff management's order to vacate the premises. Matters reach a climax at noon today when, after apparently exhausting every other available method for removing Woodside from their property, the Seacliff company called on the sheriff's office for aid.

Responding to the Seacliff request Sheriff Trafton, accompanied by Under Sheriff Rountree, proceeded to the Woodside house. Here is related, the officers' demand of Woodside that he comply with the order to vacate, was met with a volley from the alleged squatter's pistol, shot twice through the abdomen, Dick Rountree crumpled to the ground. Woodside then turned his gun on Sheriff Trafton, the latter official falling hit with the bullet only an inch or two below his heart on his left side.

Sept. 5.—Predi der military arre ays, Col. Willia 8th corps area, a denunciation of t connection wi e Shenandoah a an attempted b

In 1925 on the cliffs above Seacliff Beach, a recluse named Paul Woodside was approached by Sheriff Howard A. Trafton (inset, right) and undersheriff Dick Rountree, who planned to serve him with commitment papers. In the altercation that followed, both Trafton and Woodside were killed; Rountree was wounded and later died. Woodside had refused to sell his property for a road-building project and threatened all trespassers who approached his shack. As researcher Phil Reader has noted, however, there is much more to the Woodside case than meets the eye. First, Woodside owned the property he occupied, however unsightly, and it happened to be in the way of a planned luxury housing development on the clifftop. Was Woodside dangerously insane or merely eccentric and pushed too far by forces that wanted him out of the way? Was Howard Trafton too "quick on the trigger"? Could the deaths have been prevented? And what was the role of Judge Bias, who issued the arrest order? He had an obvious conflict of interest, since his family was on the board of the Seacliff Corporation, the agency that stood to profit by developing the area. The houses were built, and today's beach access road runs right over the site.

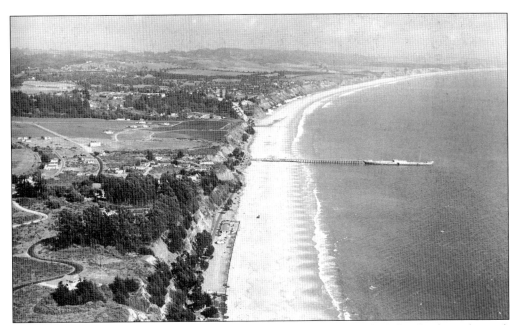

Paul Woodside's view was well worth preserving; this is the area in which his shack was located. In fact, Woodside left a manuscript of a book he commenced in 1923, described in the *Santa Cruz Evening News* as "a story of adventure" filled with appreciative descriptions of his environs. The beachfront area developed relatively late (in the 1920s) as an upscale retreat area for San Francisco visitors. Rio del Mar is in the background, with the concrete ship and pier at center.

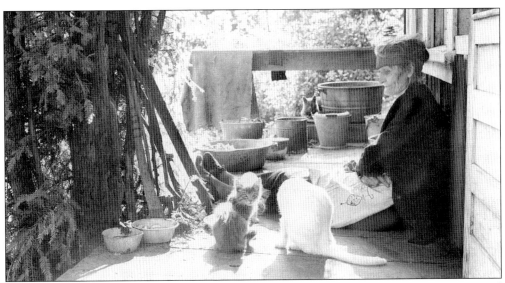

"Mother Alice" Benninghoven (1863–1944), religionist, philosopher, and writer, is pictured here at her isolated Skyland home. A sign in front of her property reads, "New Jerusalem Colony," but in fact she lived a solitary and ascetic life. Her habit of wearing sheets, sandals, and a turban did not endear her to her neighbors and prompted wild speculation among them. A manuscript account of her experiences, entitled "Religious Persecution in Skyland," describes her feud with her neighbor Hiram Ingraham, who persisted in blasting stumps on the edge of her property that pelted her home with noise and debris.

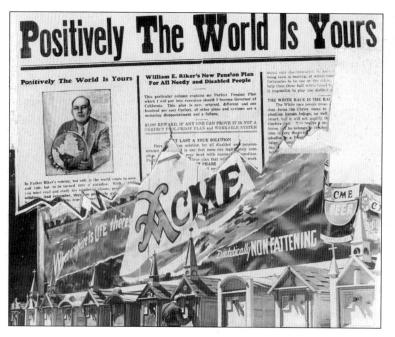

Holy City, located on the Old Santa Cruz Highway, was established by "Father" William E. Riker (1873–1969) in 1919. From a background as a huckster and sometime mystic, he created a philosophy called the Perfect Christian Divine Way. Holy City was designed as a utopian community of followers, embodying "the world's most perfect government." Riker claimed to receive messages from God through his nerves, most of which were virulently racist in character. He ran as a candidate for governor of California four times, proposing in part that "Negroes and Orientals" be denied the right to vote and the right to own or run businesses. In 1942 he was arrested for sedition for writing letters of support to Adolf Hitler; his lawyer, Melvin Belli, won him an acquittal, but enraged Riker by describing him as a "crackpot" during the trial.

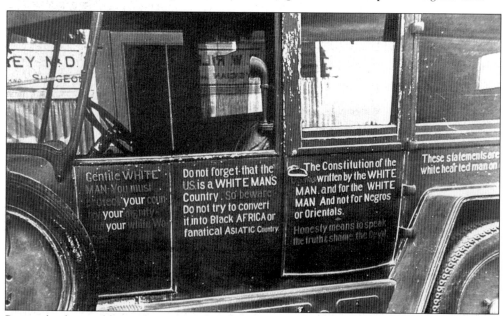

Positively the world is...whose? Far from being merely a quaint and curious artifact of the Depression Era, Holy City's Brotherhood of the Perfect Christian Divine Way advocated white supremacy and segregation in no uncertain terms. The carefully painted inscription on the car reflects the tenor of most of Riker's publications.

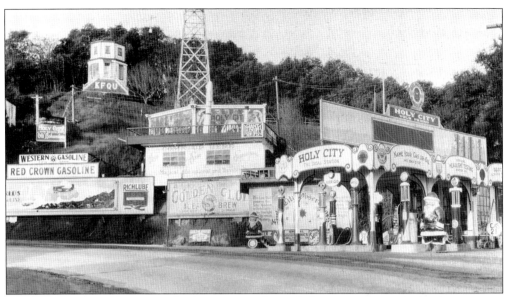

Holy City contained businesses for the tourist trade, including a gas station, barbershop, grocery store, restaurant, observatory, zoo, and radio station KFQU. In the early 1930s, Holy City attracted the out-of-work, and its population grew to 300. The opening of Highway 17 led to a drop in revenues and membership, and most of the buildings were destroyed in a series of fires in the 1960s.

This is an unmistakable view of the Garfield Park vicinity on the west side of Santa Cruz. "The Circles" neighborhood stands out clearly from the air, although the site of the tabernacle at the circles' center stands empty in this view. In this photo, Garfield Park's main street (once Garfield, now Woodrow Avenue) leads from the front door of the church directly to the cliffs. In the eight o'clock position is Bay Street, which meets

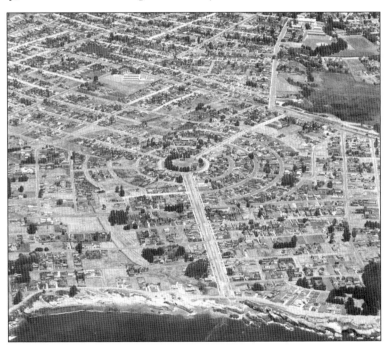

California Street at Neary Lagoon. This area was once the home of the state Christian Churches conference site, which laid out the area with its tabernacle at the center, surrounded by cottages and tent lots for conference attendees. The original church was octagonal in shape, with a 100-foot tower; built in 1890, it stood for 45 years before it was lost to fire in 1935. The outlying streets that ringed the tabernacle were named for prominent church workers.

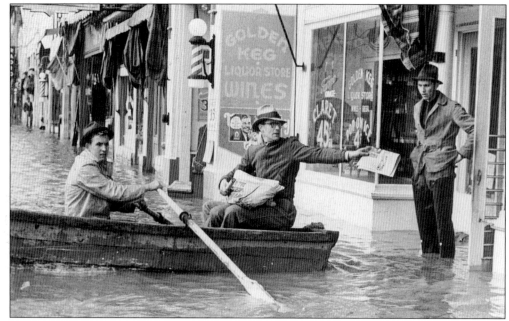

Pictured is Main Street near City Hall during the Watsonville flood of February 11 and 12, 1938. After 15 days of rain, on February 12, the storm-swollen main Watsonville levee broke at 6:30 a.m., inundating Watsonville and Pajaro. The longest rainy period on record up to that date, the rain was accompanied by hurricane-force winds that uprooted trees and ripped off rooftops in Santa Cruz as well.

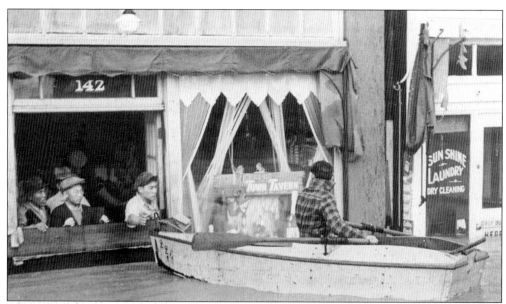

Pictured is Satoru Kokka Grocery at 142 Main Street during 1938 flood. Most of the town of Pajaro and sections of Watsonville, including two blocks of its business district, were flooded and business establishments barricaded their doors to prevent flooding of the buildings. As the *Santa Cruz Evening News* reported, "In the low-lying Pajaro district many of the Oriental quarters were swamped, with likelihood that many families would have to abandon their homes."

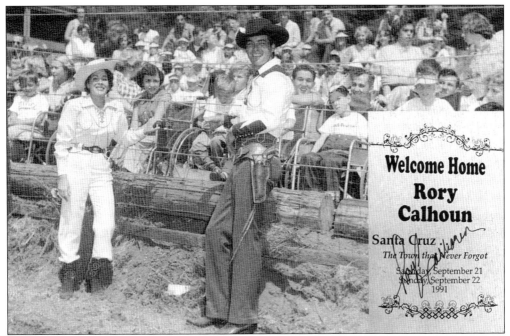

Welcome Home
Rory
Calhoun

Santa Cruz
The Town that Never Forgot
Saturday, September 21
Sunday, September 22
1991

Rory Calhoun (1922–1999), actor best known for his many roles in Western television shows and movies, lived in Santa Cruz between 1927 and 1936, returning in 1939 to attend Santa Cruz High School. He held jobs at Santa Cruz Lumber in Boulder Creek and the Division of Forestry office in Felton; he was also a longboard surfer and rodeo participant. In 1991 he was honored with a "return to Santa Cruz" program (inset).

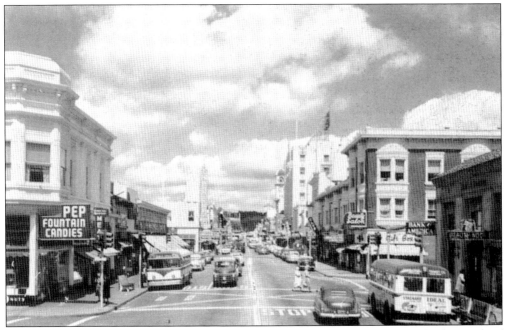

This postcard captured downtown in 1953 at Pacific and Lincoln and Soquel. The Bank of America is on the right, and the Pep Creamery Fountain is on the corner at left.

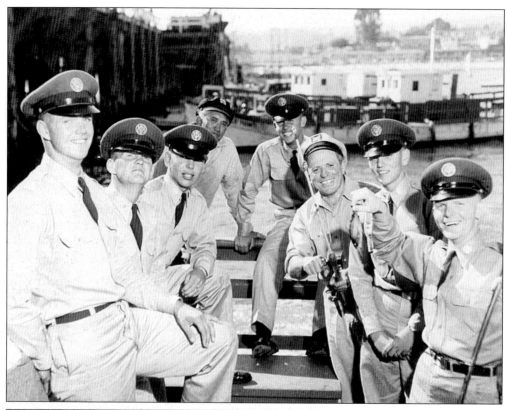

At the start of World War II, many local boys in the Santa Cruz fishing community were already in the Navy Reserves. Sixth from left is Malio J. Stagnaro (*b.* 1900), member of an early Santa Cruz fishing family. Stagnaro's oral history, recorded by UCSC in 1973, provides a wealth of detail about the fishing industry in Monterey Bay and the Italian-American community in Santa Cruz.

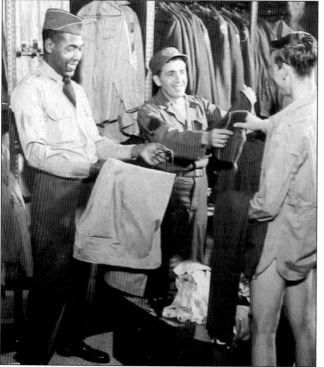

Pictured here, from left to right, are Cornelius "Cornie" Bumpus, Sam Del Vecchio, and Pvt. Edward J. Hagan at a military clothing sale.

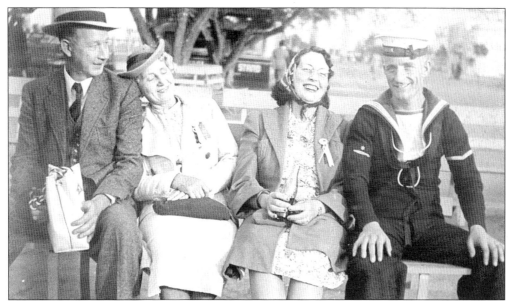

Elmer Park (far left) was a printer who worked for the *Santa Cruz Sentinel* for over 50 years. His wife Violet (third from left) owned Vi Park's Camera Shop on Walnut Avenue. Both died in the 1960s. The other two members of this pleasant group are unidentified.

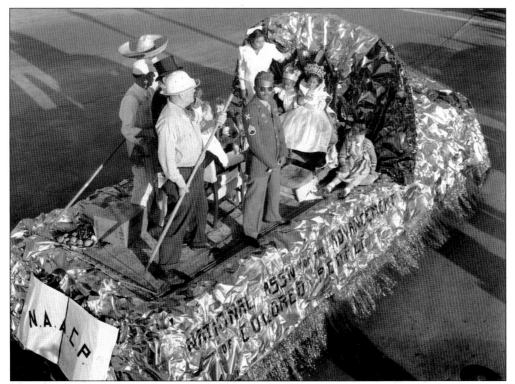

This is an NAACP float at the Santa Cruz Fiesta Days Parade, late 1940s. The float was designed to draw attention to the wartime service of African Americans. (Photo courtesy of Covello & Covello)

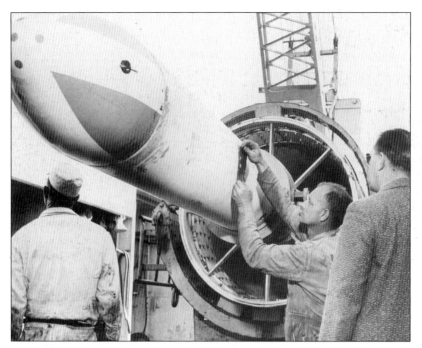

A mysterious presence in the Santa Cruz mountains for years, Lockheed Martin Missiles & Space Division has had a test base on Empire Grade Road, a few miles up the road from UCSC in Bonny Doon. Lockheed develops and tests components of missile systems on the site; the Navy is its main customer. The road along the ridgetop past the turnoff for Bonny Doon dead-ends at the 3,700 acre gated facility, which has scaled back operations considerably in recent years. This photo was taken in the mid-1950s, an era more friendly to defense industry boosterism.

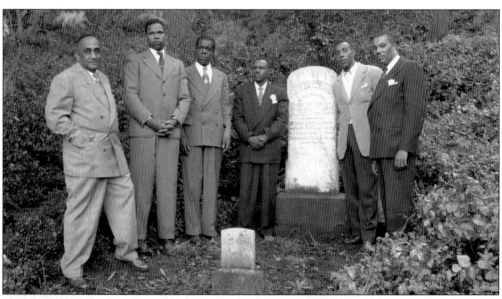

In February 1953, the Santa Cruz Chapter of the NAACP honored the memory of Louden (London) Nelson, a freed slave who willed his property to the Santa Cruz public school district. Nelson died on May 17, 1860. The two-room school across from Nelson's Water Street property had been abandoned for lack of funds in 1859, and his gift revitalized the struggling school district. He is buried in Evergreen Cemetery. (Photo courtesy of Covello & Covello)

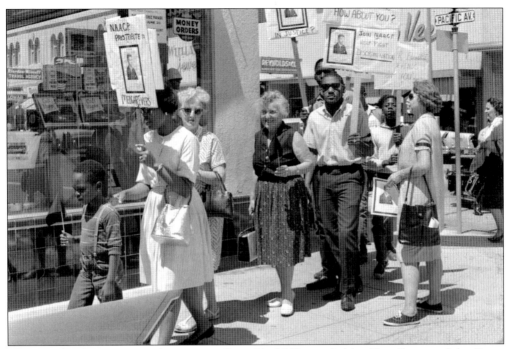

This march of mourning and protest on June 21, 1963, was led by Gary Bowen of the Santa Cruz chapter of the NAACP Youth Council to honor the memory of slain NAACP Field Secretary Medgar Evers. Evers had died a week earlier in Jackson, Mississippi. (Photo courtesy of Covello & Covello)

Londoner Vic Jowers and his wife Sidney opened the Sticky Wicket restaurant in Santa Cruz in 1958, later moving its location to Aptos adjacent to Highway 1. The restaurant and coffee house was known for its "Beat" atmosphere; it offered chamber music concerts, an art gallery, and a reading room. Later, its "New Vic" outdoor theater became the catalyst for the Cabrillo

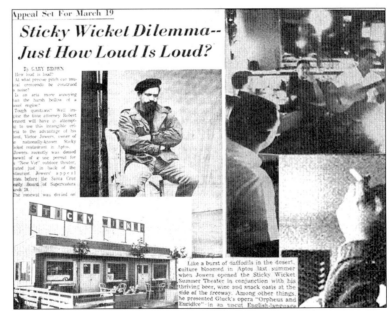

Music Festival. Complaints about noise and traffic, and the construction of a new overpass that cut off easy access to the Sticky Wicket hastened its demise in 1962. Scrapbooks and other memorabilia related to the Sticky Wicket are now in the UCSC collections.

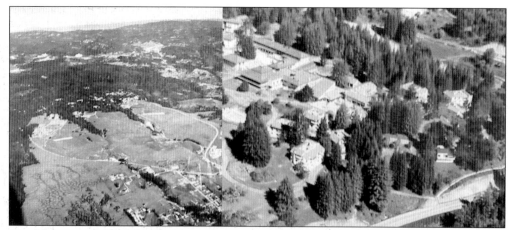

The University of California, Santa Cruz campus was formerly the site of the Cowell Lime Company. The campus was planned in the 1960s as a cluster of colleges grouped around separate courtyards, with care to preserve the natural setting; it opened in 1965. At left, an aerial view of the new campus; at right, a closer view of one of the original colleges. The Santa Cruz of the post-UCSC 1960s mixed the existing retiree-dominated town with a politically active "counterculture" student community. Both groups were drawn by the then-inexpensive place with year-round good weather, but their ideologies often put them at odds.

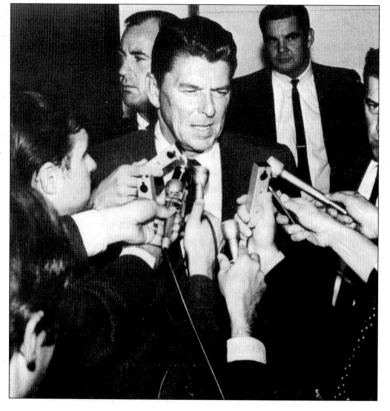

Then-Governor Ronald Reagan visited UCSC in the fall of 1968 for a meeting of the Board of Regents. Student demonstrations centering on issues including the UFW Grape Boycott were held to coincide with the visit. Al Crawley, the brand-new UCSC staff member assigned to "keep an eye on things" (pictured to the right of Mr. Reagan) recalls that the mood was ugly that day, and that the event was a dramatic introduction to the political climate of the new campus.

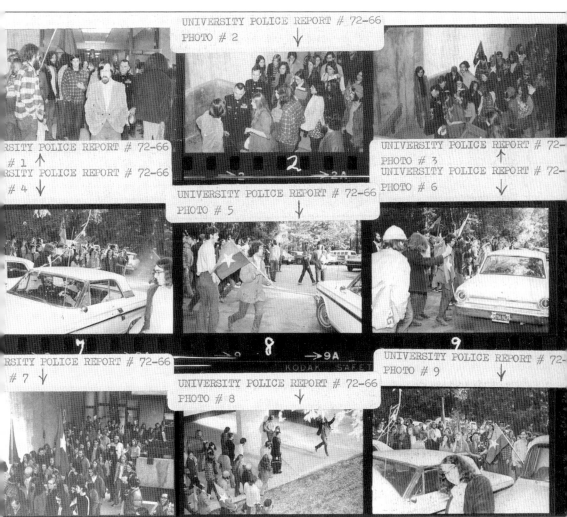

On May 19, 1969, UCSC students protested Governor Ronald Reagan's calling out the National Guard at the UC Berkeley campus; on May 15, disputes over the property known as People's Park had reached the exploding point. The protest at UCSC, involving a blockade of the Central Services building, was nonviolent.

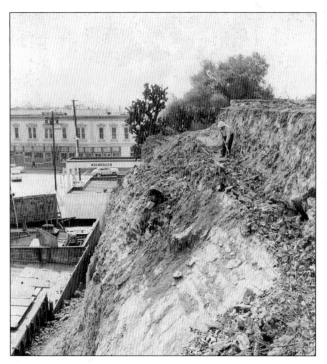

Photographs of downtown often originate from this view spot, an unstable cliff above Pacific Avenue on Mission Hill, which has plagued businesses below it for years. One long-time local restaurant had a chunk of this cliff fall on it, destroying the building; it moved to a fancier location inside the Cooperhouse on Pacific Avenue. Only months later, the Loma Prieta earthquake destroyed the Cooperhouse and the restaurant had to move again. Its owner noted its grand reopening with a cartoon in the local papers depicting a meteor streaking though space, and the words, "somewhere, in the universe, a meteor is changing course..." The building in the background is significant for many locals who remember the old McHugh & Bianchi Grocery Store, lost to "progress" in the early 1970s despite a lengthy and bitter fight to save it. An orange stucco bank building replaced it. Some say the loss galvanized the community, which has since tended to be resistant to developing historical sites and open spaces. One gable of the old building was given to the UCSC library, where it is displayed, along with one of the Cooperhouse bricks.

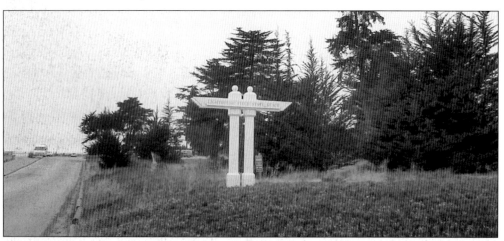

Lighthouse Field State Beach, which encompasses Lighthouse Point and Lighthouse Field, is one of the last open headlands in a California urban area. It is one of the places where Monarch butterflies winter along the coast. In the 1970s, the 10+ acres of Lighthouse Field were destined to be the site of a conference center and hotel, which spurred the formation of local environmental groups and the eventual abandonment of the project. Similarly, a planned beach traffic loop linking Highway 1, Highway 17, and the Boardwalk was blocked by low growth and environmental advocates.

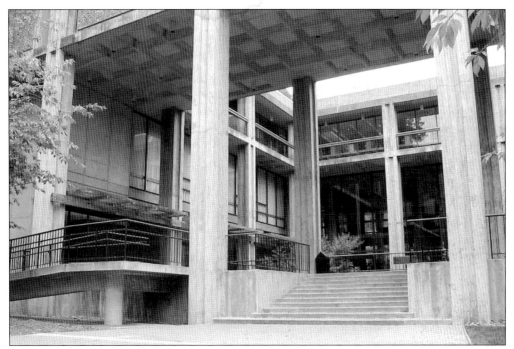

McHenry Library at UCSC houses the originals of most of the images in this book. The founding university librarian, Donald Thomas Clark, fought hard to retain the atrium as a focal point of the library building, though state architects wanted to eliminate it. In 1983, the president of the University named this feature "The Donald T. Clark Courtyard."

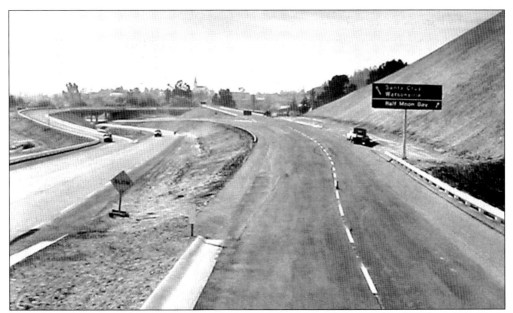

This image is included as a gift to our readers who, like us, travel the overburdened road that runs the length of our community. This is the view approaching the intersection locals know as "the fishhook," taken when the road was new. It is tempting to say it's a little nicer to look at now, but, despite the lack of landscaping, there is something to be said for all that clear asphalt.

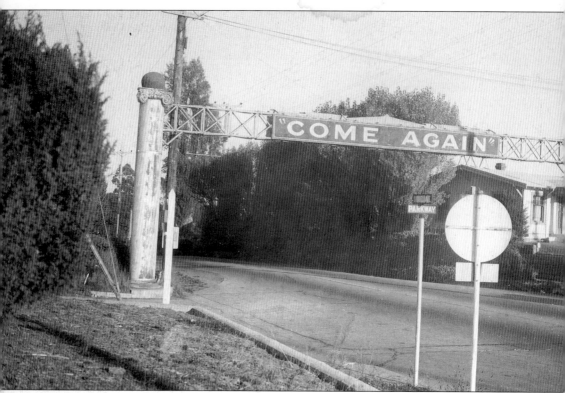

The "Come Again" exit sign at the city limits, Soquel Avenue and Park Way, is now the site of a car dealership. Welcome signs may be no more than advertising, but a sign to say goodbye is a gracious thing. While a single departure point from Santa Cruz would now be difficult to place, the community continues to welcome both visitors and those who call it home. Welcome to Santa Cruz—and come again.